Reckless Speculation about Murder

Barney Doyle

Genius
Book Services

Los Angeles, California

Published by:
Genius Book Publishing
31858 Castaic Road #154
Castaic, CA 91384

ISBN: 978-1-947521-24-7

Library of Congress Control Number: 2020935092

200316

Contents

Dedicated to my loving wife, my two wonderful boys, my fantastic family and to one of the two poorly-trained dogs living in my house. They know which one.

Reckless Speculation about Murder

Introduction

I can tell by the way you bought this book that you and I are going to get along great. You have wonderful taste and you have enough money to purchase a book. I only know two things about you so far and I'm already impressed. We're going to do some incredible work together.

It won't be hard work. And it isn't terribly important work. And there will be no pay. But it is extremely fun work. At least fun for people like you and me. We are going to solve murders.

We won't "solve" them in the legal sense. That *is* hard work. I'm not swabbing mysterious carpet stains and you aren't filling out photo logs or chain-of-custody labels. Neither of us is going to swear out an affidavit or testify in a hearing. That crap is boring. We're going to "solve" murders in the literary sense. We are going to review the hard work that other people have already done, use our powerful intellects to draw logical inferences, and then boldly proclaim solutions that won't ever suffer the scrutiny of a court of law.

Maybe a few internet know-it-alls will say hurtful things about our work on Reddit, but pay no mind to them. They are just jealous of your wonderful taste and your book money.

At this point, I can tell you are excited. You're ready to go. You've got yourself a cup of coffee (is that schnapps I smell?), you've got a notebook beside you, and you muted Forensic Files in the background. You are ready to solve some murders. But you're probably also wondering why you can't just do this on your own. After all, you're the one with the wonderful taste. You're the one with the discretionary income. What do you need old Barney Doyle for anyway?

Well, that's an awkward question to ask this early in a partnership, but I get it. Skepticism is critical when you are solving murders and I couldn't trust you as a partner if you weren't a little skeptical about me. So let me explain what I bring to this relationship.

First of all, this book is about 55,000 words long. I challenge you to find more than 1,000 typos, errors or grammatical mistakes. 54,000 out of 55,000 words spelled and used correctly. That's 98% accuracy. Michael Jordan scored less than 33,000 points in his career and that was on 51% shooting. I'm basically a greater word speller than Michael Jordan was a basketball player. If you see a word in this book you can be 98% sure that it is spelled correctly and means what I think it means.

Also, I actually did solve murders for a living. In the legal sense. I was an actual homicide investigator. I've processed crime scenes. I've interrogated suspects. I've sworn out affidavits and testified in court hearings. I wasn't a world-renowned expert on anything, by any means, but I was a competent criminal investigator who put people in prison. That isn't exactly what we are doing here, but it's similar.

Also, I am pretty good at filtering out bullshit and nonsense. That is going to be very important for the task at hand. I don't have access to any insider information in these cases, so we are solving these things with only the information that is available to the general public. Misinformation and misleading information could sabotage our efforts. However, I am familiar with police reports, medical reports and court records. I have a pretty good understanding of what weight should be given to all of the different types of evidence. I know what hearsay is and can evaluate when it has value. The cases that we will be looking at are blanketed in layers of b.s. and nonsense. I'll cull through that mess and find the facts that we can actually rely on.

Given that, your wonderful taste and all that extra cash, I'd say we are a pretty formidable crime solving duo. Maybe not Nancy Drew, but I'd stack our work against anything the Hardy Boys have ever done. Any day of the week. And I'm not just saying that so you'll throw a little more of that cash at a sequel.

The Murder of Teresa Halbach

Before we go on, I should warn you that I am going to spend some portion of this book ridiculing criminal attorneys. I can't help it. They are a ridiculous group of people. They are among the most educated and intelligent people we have in this country and have devoted their lives to civil service. They should be revered like doctors or astronauts, but instead they are derided like old-timey carnival barkers. The burden of proof is entirely on their shoulders, yet prosecutors are mocked as buffoons if they lose a case. Prosecutors who are too successful are portrayed as heartless henchmen for an oppressive government machine. Defense attorneys are villainized for protecting criminals even though we all understand it is their exact job to protect the rights of their clients, who are mostly criminals, and they would be disbarred for giving anything less than an honest effort.

But that's the job they chose and most of the absurdities of the criminal justice system were created by their hands. They stacked one absurd brief or motion on top of another for two centuries until our courts were trapped in a slog of arcane case laws and nonsensical gibberish that only lawyers and sovereign citizens pretend to understand. I'll give you a couple of observations from a decade I have spent as an occasional guest of the court: The judge is God in the courtroom, but God's will can always be appealed to a council of higher deities; logic is suspended for the sake of ritual; and at least three jurors haven't paid attention to a word the last witness just said.

Since I know that I am a weak man who will take numerous unprovoked shots at the attorneys involved in these cases, I do feel compelled to admit a couple of important things that I have noticed about attorneys. In their own little way, they always seem to tell the truth. I've seen doctors lie. I've seen clergy lie. I've seen my mother lie. I can't recall seeing an attorney lie in court. Despite their reputation to the contrary, as a whole, attorneys seem to have a real commitment to their own narrow concept of truth. That's not to say that they won't mislead the shit out of you with an argument, because they will absolutely do that. But you can be sure that the argument is based on some truthful fact. Listening to attorneys is a lot like negotiating with the devil. They aren't going to lie to you, but pay very close attention to the words they choose. Second, they tend to be much better mannered than you expect a professional arguer to be. I've heard horror stories about attorneys being jerks to witnesses on the stand but I've never actually seen it. I've always been treated with respect and decency when I testified. I've had my work criticized by defense attorneys while I was on the stand and that stung. But they were never jerks about it and the criticisms were always reasonably valid (probably why they stung).

So there you are, that's a quick guide to attorneys from Barney Doyle. They virtually always tell the truth, even if only in a very literal and lawyerly sense of the word "truth," and they aren't nearly as bad as all of the jokes would have you believe.

I say all of that because we are going to talk about the tragic murder of Teresa Halbach and we can't do that without reviewing the trial of Steven Avery. The defense attorneys who represented Avery, Dean Strang and Jerome Buting, became a pair of modern day Atticus Finches to a throng of worshipers on the internet after a flattering portrayal in the Netflix documentary *Making a Murderer*. The prosecutor, Ken Kratz, resigned in disgrace over allegations that he made unwanted sexual advances towards several victims in domestic violence cases that he was prosecuting.

In Avery's trial, each side presented a theory on this case and the two theories were mutually exclusive. Lots of times in a murder trial the defense won't present a theory, they will just poke holes in the prosecutor's theory. Other times the defense will accept the bulk of the prosecutor's theory without argument and try to insert doubt through insanity, self-defense, accident or some other gray area in the law. The Steven Avery trial was the rare case where the prosecution and the defense offered specific theories that directly contradicted each other. One of them, at a minimum, has to be wrong. What we think happened to Teresa Halbach depends largely on who we are going to believe, the modern day Misters Finch or an alleged sexual predator. I know whose side you want to take on this one. Hell, I know whose side I want to take on this one. But as I mentioned before, attorneys virtually always tell the truth in court. So let's wade through all of this contradictory truth and see if we can't figure out what actually happened.

Also, before we go any further, I want you to take a moment and consider your own interest in these cases. I love true crime stories. You love true crime stories. Lots of people love true crime stories. There is nothing wrong with loving true crime stories. The subject matter is macabre, but that doesn't make it off limits for decent people like us to discuss. We don't love murder and we certainly don't want to celebrate murderers. If anything, our love of true crime is mostly borne of an obsession with finding the truth and holding murderers accountable. The crimes we are going to look at, like the murder of Teresa Halbach, were devastating events to a lot of innocent people who cared about the victims. And that is before you even account for the horrors that the poor victims themselves suffered. We recognize the tragedy, hate the suffering, and love the story still. We are searching for the truth among muddied details in most of these cases, but we are never confused about where our sympathies lie. The victim is the most important person in every one of these stories. Even though we enjoy studying these crimes, we still wish they had not happened in the first place.

And I know a lot of you developed your interest in these things in relation to some personal tragedy in your own life. Studying horrific crimes is, for some people, a coping mechanism for dealing with trauma. I've seen more death and violence in my life than I ever imagined I could handle. These murder stories should stir up a lot of terrible memories for me. But they don't. They allow me to dissect the horrors of this world from a comfortable arm's length away, secure in the knowledge that I can always just close the book or the laptop at any time. It's a weird way of distracting yourself from the boogieman under your bed by reading about the boogieman three states over. It shouldn't work, but it does.

That said, we all have those true crime cases that hit too close to home. If any of these cases are like that for you, or if, God forbid, you personally knew one of the victims, please just skip that chapter. You won't miss anything important, I promise, and you'll catch up on the next case.

Also, now is an appropriate time to offer my sincere thanks to Skip Topp and his friends over at stevenaverycase. org for compiling the trial transcripts and all of the supporting exhibits from the Steven Avery trial. Trial transcripts are public records but are usually prohibitively expensive, so I am very grateful that they acquired and shared them. The facts below come from those transcripts, several other motions filed by attorney Kathleen Zellner and, to a much lesser extent, the *Making a Murderer* documentary.

Teresa Halbach was a 25-year-old photographer living in semi-rural Wisconsin. She was relatively new to the business so she shared studio space with another photographer and supplemented her income by doing freelance photography for an Auto Trader magazine. If you aren't familiar with Auto Trader, picture Craigslist car ads compiled in a free newspaper that was available in a filthy display box outside of every gas station. If you aren't familiar with newspapers, imagine printing a collection of articles from the internet onto awkwardly large and absurdly thin paper that you could take with you to the bathroom. If you don't remember articles, they were like memes but with 800 to 1,000 words and sometimes no picture.

On Halloween day of 2005, Teresa Halbach was taking photos of vehicles for three different customers in and around Manitowoc County, Wisconsin. One of those customers was a man named Steven Avery who lived in a trailer at the Avery Salvage Yard. Everybody agrees that Teresa visited the Avery Salvage Yard that day. And everybody agrees that Teresa's burned remains were found in a burn pit behind Steven Avery's home several days later. But what happened between those moments is fiercely debated.

The prosecution's version of events:

Teresa Halbach had taken photos at the Avery Salvage Yard on several occasions before. She complained to a coworker about Steven Avery's peculiar behavior. She said that Avery once met her at the door wearing nothing but a towel.

On October 31, 2005, Avery called Auto Trader magazine and specifically requested that Teresa come take photos. Avery gave the Avery Salvage Yard address, but gave the name B. Janda instead of his own. Avery's sister's name was Barb Janda and the vehicle that Teresa was supposed to photograph belonged to her. Avery had Teresa's cell phone number and called her twice before she came out to the salvage yard. Both times he used *67 to block his name and number on her caller ID. She didn't answer either call. He called again later in the day, presumably after her visit, but did not use *67 on the third call.

Bobby Dassey lived in a trailer at the Avery Salvage Yard with his mother (Barb Janda) and brothers. He saw Teresa taking photos of his mother's van that afternoon, then saw Teresa walking toward Avery's trailer. Bobby took a shower and left to go hunting. He saw Teresa's green Toyota RAV4 parked out at the property but did not see Teresa anywhere when he left.

Multiple witnesses reported seeing a bonfire and/or a fire in a burn barrel at Steven Avery's residence on the afternoon and/or evening of October 31. The statements conflict as to the exact time of the fires, but consensus seems to place them at around dusk into dark.

Friends and loved ones did not see or hear from Teresa after October 31, and her mother reported her as a missing person on November 3 in Calumet County Wisconsin, where Teresa lived. Police accounted for her whereabouts up to the point where she visited the Avery Salvage Yard, then the trail went cold.

A large search party of citizen volunteers, organized by Teresa's ex-boyfriend and her roommate, combed the countryside looking for Teresa and her missing Toyota RAV4. Teresa's second cousin located the RAV4 semi-concealed among the junk vehicles in the Avery Salvage Yard. The car was locked and partially covered with debris.

Police were notified and responded immediately. The Manitowoc County Sheriff's Office was on scene first, but the investigation was turned over to the Calumet County Sheriff's Office because of a conflict of interest. Standby for details on the conflict of interest because it makes up the bulk of the defense's theory.

The RAV4 was hauled off on a wrecker to the Wisconsin crime lab. Lab technicians found Avery's blood on the back of the gear shift and on the passenger side of the center console. His DNA, from a non-blood source, was also found under the hood on the latching mechanism. A small amount of Teresa's blood and hair was also found in the rear cargo area of the RAV4.

Through a series of searches over the course of several weeks, investigators found Teresa's bone fragments in a burn pit outside of Steven Avery's trailer and in a burn barrel outside of the Janda home. They also found charred remnants of Teresa's camera and cell phone in a burn barrel outside of Steven Avery's trailer. Inside the trailer, investigators found a key to Teresa's RAV4 in Avery's bedroom and a fired bullet with Teresa's DNA on it in the garage. The key also had Avery's DNA on it.

Investigators interviewed Avery's nephew, Brendan Dassey, several times over the course of a few months. He initially denied knowledge of what happened to Teresa, but eventually confessed to helping Avery rape and kill Teresa then burn her corpse.

The defense's version of events:

An adult female (not Teresa) was brutally raped on a beach in Manitowoc County on July 29, 1985. DNA eventually showed that the rape was almost certainly committed by a man named Gregory Allen. But a poor investigation and a mistaken eyewitness identification led to the wrongful conviction of Steven Avery.

Avery was freed in September of 2003 and rightfully sued the bejeezus out of the Manitowoc County Sheriff's Office. Either by winning the lawsuit or by agreeing to an out-of-court settlement, Avery was going to receive a huge settlement from the Manitowoc County Sheriff's Office after 20 years in prison for a rape he didn't commit. Circumstances changed when Teresa Halbach went missing the same day she visited the Avery Salvage Yard.

Among the officers deposed in Avery's lawsuit against Manitowoc County were Lieutenant James Lenk and Sergeant Andrew Colborn. Even though the investigation was turned over to the Calumet County Sheriff's Office,

Lenk and Colborn each participated in searches in which crucial evidence was discovered.

As is custom, investigators kept a log of everybody who came in and out of the crime scene at the salvage yard. There was one day when Lenk signed out of the scene log, but there was no entry for him signing in.

The RAV4 was found parked with the battery disconnected. There was a car crusher at the salvage yard not far from where it was located. The car crusher did not belong to the Averys, but they were known to use it on occasion.

One day prior to the actual discovery of the RAV4, Sergeant Colborn ran a license plate check of the vehicle through his dispatch. The majority of license plate checks are conducted by radio, but Sergeant Colborn ran this particular license plate check by cell phone. Hold on to this fact. It will become important in a moment.

Steven Avery's trailer was searched three separate times before the key to Teresa's RAV4 was discovered in his bedroom. It was discovered by Lenk and Colborn, who were searching under the supervision of a Calumet County detective. Lenk spotted the key on some slippers. Colborn theorized that the key had fallen out of a small bookshelf while he was moving it. The key was also by itself, with no accompanying house keys or office keys.

The bullet with Teresa's DNA was not discovered until months after the first search, and was discovered by Lenk. The garage had been searched multiple times before that, including a search that yielded fired .22 cartridge cases (or shell casings, as the cool kids call them).

The lab technician who identified Teresa's DNA on the bullet deviated from her usual protocol on the test. Whenever technicians test for DNA, they also run a simultaneous "control" test to show that there was no contamination. On that particular control test, the sample was contaminated with the technician's DNA. That usually isn't a big deal. They throw out the test and try again. But the DNA test on the bullet consumed the entire sample, so she was unable to run another test. In all probability, the test shouldn't have been considered valid for court purposes.

There was already a vial of Steven Avery's blood in a box of evidence at the Manitowoc County Clerk of Court's office. The Manitowoc County Sheriff's Office had keys to the Clerk's office, and Lenk was aware that evidence in Steven Avery's original rape case was held there because he had previously ordered one of his deputies to send some evidence from that box to the crime lab for testing. The vial appeared to have been opened at some point.

The vial of Avery's blood had an anticoagulant called EDTA in it that is used to preserve blood samples in liquid form. The FBI tested Avery's blood from the SUV and determined that it did not have EDTA in it, which would seem to refute the notion that the blood in the SUV was planted by law enforcement. The FBI only tested three of the six samples from the SUV, however. And the defense would introduce an expert who suggested that there were problems with the test that the FBI used.

Teresa's bones were discovered in both the burn pit in Avery's backyard and a burn barrel near the Janda residence.

There was also a third site near the Avery property where burned bones were discovered, but the crime lab was unable to determine if they were also bones from Teresa. At a minimum, either Teresa was dismembered and burned at two sites, or her burned bones were moved at least once before they were discovered.

The Avery Salvage Yard also had a commercial incinerator on site. It was not used to dispose of Teresa's body.

Before we continue, I want to tell you a little story. I am not particularly handy but I am very cheap. Consequently, I do a lot of projects around the house that should be hired out to the professionals. I built a laundry room one time that didn't have a straight edge or 90-degree angle in it. It wasn't obvious to the naked eye, so I didn't really care. Until I tried to buy a door. Door manufacturers make a lot of different sizes, but they are virtually all perfect rectangles. My opening was not. I shimmed and jimmied it every which way I could, but you can only be so precise when you don't have straight edge to orient off of. It's in the wall now, but I don't trust that door to hold out a stiff draft.

The prosecution and the defense both have timelines for when they say Teresa was at the Avery Salvage yard, but they are built on imprecise and contradictory witness recollections. I don't have any more faith in their timelines than I do in my laundry room door.

So now that we've laid that groundwork, let's do a little reckless speculation about what happened to Teresa Halbach.

I love the care and craft that went into Dean Strang and Jerome Buting's defense. A man wrongfully convicted of a rape he didn't commit is released from prison only to be framed for murder. Lieutenant Lenk is lurking in the shadows of every search with another piece of fraudulent evidence. His henchman, Sergeant Colborn, covers for every misdeed in a zeal to preserve the reputation of his beloved department. Scientists at the Wisconsin Department of Justice and the Federal Bureau of Investigation cast aside their sacred oaths to jump into the conspiracy. Maybe the police are protecting the real killers. Maybe the police are the real killers. I love everything about this story. As fiction, it's a winner. As an actual explanation for what happened to Teresa Halbach, it just doesn't work for me.

It sucks that the Manitowoc County Sheriff's Office participated in the investigation. They wouldn't have asked Calumet County to take over the investigation if they didn't believe there was a conflict of interest. Ideally they shouldn't have even participated in the search. But practically speaking, they had to. It was a ridiculously large crime scene. The Avery Salvage Yard is 5 acres with over 4,000 vehicles and a dozen buildings. The Calumet County Sheriff's Office was a 30-officer department trying to run a massive investigation in somebody else's county. You could search that salvage yard around the clock for a week with a hundred trained investigators and not cover everything. Conflict of interest or not, Manitowoc County was going to have to lend a hand in that search.

James Lenk and Andrew Colborn did not have any reason to frame Steven Avery. They weren't being sued. They had nothing to do with the investigation that led to Avery's wrongful conviction. Neither man even worked for the Manitowoc County Sheriff's Office at that time. They were deposed in Avery's lawsuit because a phone call from a neighboring agency about Avery was misdirected to Colborn while Colborn was working in the jail. He properly directed the caller to the Sheriff's Office detectives and had no further involvement in the matter. Lenk was deposed because Colborn told Lenk about the phone call. Neither man was at the slightest risk of being held personally liable in a lawsuit from Avery.

You could argue that loyalty to the Manitowoc County Sheriff's Office might motivate Lenk and Colborn to frame an innocent man. You could argue that, if you enjoy losing arguments. Police don't give a shit about their departments. It's just an employer. The job is dangerous. It doesn't pay that well. And police jobs are a dime a dozen. No police officer in the world is going to commit a felony to protect the reputation of their department or save the department from a lawsuit. Certain unscrupulous police officers might be willing to commit a felony to protect their own reputation or save themselves from a lawsuit, but not the department. Especially in a sheriff's office, where the top guy is some politician that half the department didn't even vote for and who could be gone at the next election.

But since we are recklessly speculating here, let's follow this thread a little ways. If Steven Avery didn't kill

Teresa Halbach, then who did? She didn't have a boyfriend that we know of. Her ex-boyfriend, Ryan Hillegas, was still in her life in some capacity and would make for an obvious suspect. For reasons that aren't entirely clear to me in reviewing the trial transcripts, the investigating officers ruled Hillegas out as a suspect fairly early in the investigation. I found a lot written about him on the internet, but nothing from any source that I would consider credible.

Avery hired attorney Kathleen Zellner to represent him on his appeal, which took place after his *Making a Murderer* fame. She has been very bold in proclaiming Hillegas as the actual killer. I wish I could afford to hire this woman to write the forward for this book. She is a marvel. You and I do a decent job of recklessly speculating about murders; Zellner is a master at it. Where we are bound by logic and decency, Zellner transcends reason and scoffs at decorum. We trust experts who have studied science while she directs doctors who invent science to conform to her theories. We are skeptical of witness statements that can't be corroborated. She tells you exactly who is lying, why they are lying, and why anything that contradicts her theory is also a lie. We restrict logical inferences to only those things which can be logically inferred, and then we dampen those inferences with an acknowledgment of their uncertainty. Zellner can draw you a straight line from Teresa Halbach's murder to Ryan Hillegas' guilt using any small witness statement or piece of evidence and her own unique brand of deductive reasoning.

At the risk of infuriating Avery's supporters by shortchanging the "newly discovered evidence," I am going to abridge Zellner's theory for you here:

Ryan Hillegas was a jealous and abusive boyfriend. None of Teresa Halbach's friends or family ever mentioned anything about Hillegas being abusive, but the guy she shared a photography studio with did. He told detectives that, years ago, Teresa mentioned having an abusive ex-boyfriend. Therefore, Hillegas is a murdering woman-beater.

Teresa Halbach had a secret life where she was taking nude photographs, sleeping with her roommate and sleeping with a married man. Hillegas killed her because he was jealous. (I couldn't find the affidavits that Zellner used to support the claims about Halbach's personal life. For what it's worth, true or not, it was shitty the way she used those "facts" to degrade the victim. And if I had to bet based on the rest of her arguments, I'll take "or not" over "true" in a landslide.)

Hillegas told investigators that damage to the brake light and bumper on Halbach's car was months old. No insurance claim was ever filed, so obviously Hillegas was lying to cover up the fact that he is a murdering liar.

Hillegas was an unemployed nurse at the time of the murder. He had the time to commit the murder (unemployed) and the advanced medical training (nurse) that would be required to plant Steven Avery's blood in Halbach's car.

The door to Avery's trailer was unlocked. We can be certain of this because Avery said so himself in an affidavit and had absolutely no reason to lie. Obviously, since the door was unlocked, Hillegas snuck into the house and used his advanced nursing training to take Avery's blood from the bathroom sink to Halbach's car to frame Avery.

There were no phone calls made from Hillegas' phone during the time of the murder (as calculated by Zellner). This was because his hands were occupied strangling Halbach to death. There were also no phone calls made at various points over the following few days because his hands were occupied with burning Halbach's body and framing Steven Avery.

Investigators took photographs of Hillegas' hands during the initial investigation. Those photographs showed scratches on the back of his left hand. Other photographs taken of Halbach during her lifetime showed that she had fingernails. Forensic pathologist Larry Blum prepared an affidavit saying that he was certain, "to a reasonable degree of scientific certainty," that the scratches were caused by fingernails. Furthermore, he believed that they were caused by Halbach's fingernails while Hillegas was strangling her. He deduced all of that from photos of Hillegas' hands and reenactments he conducted with female staff members in his office. Presumably, Zellner didn't require the doctor to carry the reenactment all the way through cremation.

Another doctor, Lawrence Farwell, has invented a technique he named "brain fingerprinting." He is a Harvard-educated neuroscientist whereas I am but a humble state-educated police officer, so I will defer to Dr. Farwell as to the matter of whether or not the brain has fingers. But through brain fingerprinting, Dr. Farwell can measure scientifically whether or not a person has knowledge of something. He measured with 99.9 percent certainty that Steven Avery didn't know how Teresa Halbach was killed. Other neuroscientists have pointed out that Dr. Farwell's claims seem farfetched and that his research doesn't really adhere to the standards of what we consider "science." But they are probably just bitter that they didn't discover all of those fingers on the brain before he did.

I can't recommend reading Zellner's motion for a retrial highly enough. She torched every single person involved with the case, including Dean Strang and Jerome Buting. My favorite passage is when she asserts matter-of-factly that Sergeant Colborn conducted a clandestine illegal search of the Avery salvage yard with Hillegas' help.

"The headlights were from Sgt. Colborn's personal vehicle and he had a friend of Ms. Halbach with him to search the Avery property without a search warrant because he did not have probable cause to be on the Avery property at that point in time."

She just flat out says that a sworn police officer committed multiple felonies as if she were pointing out that the sky was blue. Her proof? Colborn called in for a license plate check on Halbach's vehicle and he used a cell phone instead of his radio. And she could hear a voice in the background say "it's her." Colborn obviously made the call while trespassing at the Avery Salvage yard and the voice in the background couldn't have been anybody but the lying, murdering, evidence-planting Hillegas.

As you might have imagined, the judge was unpersuaded and denied Zellner's motion for a new trial.

Perhaps by the sequel you and I will be audacious enough to propose Zellner's type of fantastically imaginative speculation, but we aren't there yet. For now, let's bound our recklessness in at least the realm of plausibility.

I think that Steven Avery killed Teresa Halbach. His blood was in her vehicle. His DNA was on her hood latch. Her car key was found in Steven Avery's bedroom with Steven Avery's DNA on it. A bullet with Teresa's DNA was found in his garage and it was fired from a .22 caliber rifle that was found hanging in Steven Avery's bedroom. Her bones were found in a burn pit outside of his house. Her cell phone and camera were found in a burn barrel beside his house. Each and every piece of that evidence is pretty damning.

I know you have concerns about the integrity of some of that evidence. Rightfully so. The bullet wasn't found on the first search and it probably should have been. The story of how the key was found is a bit perplexing. It's really weird that her bones were found at multiple locations on the Avery property. I will grant you all of those things. But murder isn't a perfectly logical act and you will drive yourself mad trying to understand the how and why of every little thing the killer did. The kind of person who would brutally murder an innocent person is the kind of person who would do a lot of other peculiar stuff as well. Moving bones? It obviously made sense to the killer at the time because bones were moved. Maybe somebody moved the bones in an attempt to frame Steven

Avery for the murder. But that person would have had to stage all of the other evidence as well, and the logistics just don't seem possible to me (unless the police killed her, which is absurd). The most logical explanation I see is that Steven Avery moved the bones for reasons that probably made sense to him at the time. Steven Avery's blood was in the car because Steven Avery bled in the car. Steven Avery's DNA was on the hood latch because Steven Avery touched the hood latch when he disconnected the battery. The key was eventually found in Steven Avery's room because Steven Avery hid the key in his room. The bullet was found in the garage with Teresa's DNA on it because that's where the bullet was fired. I admit that it lacks the imagination and flair of Zellner's and Strang's theories, but it fits the facts a lot easier.

So if we accept that Steven Avery was the killer, then why did he do it? They weren't romantically involved so it wasn't a case of domestic violence. Teresa was early into her photography career while Avery was in line for a huge settlement from Manitowoc County, so robbery doesn't make any sense. Neither of them was involved in a street gang nor were they distributing narcotics. There is no reason to suspect self-defense, murder-for-hire, silencing a witness or any of the other oddball murder motives that occur in rare instances. I'm going to step out on a pretty sturdy limb and guess that it was sexually motivated. You knew that already, didn't you? One step ahead of me as usual. But just for the sake of being thorough, let's analyze it a little bit.

Making a Murderer would have you believe that Steven Avery was wrongfully convicted of rape because he looked a lot like the actual rapist and the Manitowoc County Sheriff's Office bungled the investigation. In truth, Steven Avery was wrongfully convicted of rape because he looked a lot like the actual rapist, the Manitowoc County Sheriff's Office bungled the investigation and Steven Avery's behavior made it really easy to believe that he would rape somebody.

According to a report by Kurt Chandler in *Milwaukee Magazine*, Avery was convicted of burglarizing a bar when he was 18 and burning a cat alive several months later. I haven't seen the court records or police reports from either of those charges, but they fit into the general pattern of Avery's life. In September of 1984, a neighbor reported that Avery had been harassing her for months. When she drove past his house on the road to her own home, Avery would run and stand on the side of the road naked or stand at the front of his car and masturbate in plain view.

In his report, the investigating detective noted, "He has field glasses on the house and he knows just when she will be driving past the residence. At this point he will then run out to the road and do his tricks."

In January of 1985, Avery was arrested for running a woman's vehicle off the road and pointing a rifle at her. In April of 1985 he was accused of repeatedly driving by another woman's house and shouting obscenities. In May of 1985 an 11 year old girl in a neighboring community was kidnapped and raped. Avery was never charged with the crime, but officers noted that he fit the physical description of the suspect and was identified by a witness as fishing in the area at the time. In June of 1987, Avery's wife accused him of sending threatening letters from prison. In September of 2004, one year after being released from prison, Avery's girlfriend accused him of domestic assault.

It's a tragedy that a rapist was left on the streets because of Manitowoc County's shoddy investigation. Gregory Allen, the actual rapist, was free for another ten years and committed atrocities that we likely won't ever even know about before he was eventually caught for another rape. It's infuriating. But let's be honest, there were going to be concrete and bars in Avery's future eventually anyway.

If the earlier reports of Avery's roadside self-gratification were true then it's not a stretch to think that he later developed a fixation on Teresa. The 1984 police report accuses Avery of targeting a specific female with his roadside shenanigans, going so far as to watch her house with binoculars so that he wouldn't miss her. I've never known prison to do a really good job of curing perverts of their impulses. Sometimes it does teach them to conceal those impulses better. A man waving his weiner at a woman from the side of the road could just be a few years in prison away from learning to cover himself with a towel when he attempts to shock his future victims.

You and I may disagree on this one because I seem to think it's a bigger deal than everybody else does, but I believe it is very relevant that Avery made two phone calls to Teresa using the *67 feature before she arrived at his house and one call afterward without using it. What legitimate reason would he have for blocking his number? This was in the early 2000s. I'm suspicious that a man Steven Avery's age even knew about *67. A middle-aged guy in Wisconsin in 2003 who dismantled junk vehicles for a living was not aware of *67 unless he was using it for nefarious reasons. I didn't know about *67 until 2006, and that was only because I became a police officer and saw it used for nefarious reasons. I am also nearly two decades younger than Steven Avery.

The phone call afterwards without *67 shows he had a plan. When she was reported missing and they checked her phone records, he could point to that call as proof that he hadn't made the two blocked calls earlier. Obviously that fell apart when they checked his phone records, but those things happen when simple people attempt complex crimes. I said he had a plan, but I never said it was a good one.

It is also relevant that this happened while Steven Avery's live-in girlfriend was in jail. I won't go so far as to say that it is necessarily evidence, but it is an interesting fact nonetheless. If Steven were truly innocent, how unfortunate for him that Teresa was murdered while his alibi wasn't available. But if he's guilty, of course he would plan it for a time when his girlfriend was away.

OK, I'm satisfied that Steven Avery probably killed Teresa Halbach and that it was a sexually motivated crime. Now let's get a little reckless with the speculation. Let's theorize how it happened.

The autopsy revealed two bullet defects in Teresa's skull and the .22 caliber bullet fragment located in the garage with Teresa's DNA on it was fired from a .22 rifle found in Steven Avery's bedroom. It's fair to say she was shot. But where did it happen and what led up to it?

Bobby Dassey testified that he last saw Teresa walking toward Steven Avery's trailer. Assuming she made it inside, what happened next? None of Teresa's blood was found in the trailer, so I think it's fair to say that she was not shot in the trailer. A gunshot wound to the head is bloody, even with a smaller round like a .22 caliber. I just can't envision a scenario where Steven Avery would be able to clean up all of that blood without leaving a trace. If she was on carpet when she was shot, the blood would have soaked into the carpet pad and the subfloor. Even if she were on linoleum or tile, the blood would have spread over such a large area that it would almost certainly have made it into cracks and crevices that Avery wouldn't have been able to clean. And that isn't even factoring in the spatter that would have hit the walls. It is really hard and requires time and effort to make an indoor bloody murder scene disappear, and Avery would have been in a big hurry.

The bullet with Teresa's DNA was found in the garage so it makes sense that she was shot in there. In Zellner's appeal she made a very big deal out of the fact that the bullet did not have any bone fragments embedded in it. For reasons that confound me even on multiple readings, Zellner was convinced the lack of bone material on the bullet somehow proved that Avery didn't shoot Halbach. There seem to be two pretty obvious explanations. The first being that her expert might be full of crap. The second is that the bullet found in the garage might have passed through Teresa without striking a bone. A .22 is a small and fast-moving bullet, so I doubt the round found in the garage was one of the rounds that hit Teresa in the head. Forensic pathologists have explained to me in the past that .22 caliber bullets are notorious for ricocheting off bones around the inside of a person's body without ever exiting. I have a tough time believing that a .22 caliber bullet that penetrated the skull in one spot would still have enough momentum to make it out the other side and onto the garage floor still intact. But there are a lot of places where a round could pass in and out of a human body without striking bone, and we have no idea how many times Teresa was actually shot.

So if she was shot in the garage, then that raises the question of why none of Teresa's blood was found in there. If you were to get upset with old Barney Doyle for some undoubtedly legitimate reason and punch me in the nose, I'd bleed all over the bare concrete floor in my garage where I am typing this. So as not to upset my wife and risk another punch in the nose, I'd wipe that blood puddle up with a shop rag before it stained the floor. If you came back a month later and sprayed a crime scene product called Luminol on the floor, the spot where that puddle had been would light up, especially under an alternative light source. Then you wouldn't have to hit me again, you could just point to the floor and remind me to watch my manners.

Crime scene technicians used Luminol in Steven Avery's garage and saw a stain come out that was about the right size to be from a gunshot wound to the head.

So with the same scenario as above, what if old Barney Doyle didn't feel comfortable leaving puddles of DNA everywhere and decided to clean up that blood puddle with bleach instead of just wiping it up with a shop rag? What happens if you come back a month later with a bottle of Luminol this time? The spot still lights up, but because of the bleach not the blood. Bleach kills everything in the blood that reacts with the Luminol, but the bleach itself causes a reaction.

The evidence technicians in Steven Avery's garage used a presumptive blood test on the stain and determined that it was not blood.

So what if we discussed our problems like adults and you never punched old Barney Doyle in the first place? I'm clumsy and it is a garage, so I have at various times spilled brake fluid, antifreeze, medicated shampoo and Heinz 57 sauce on the floor. You bring the Luminol over and what happens then? First, I ask where you are getting all of this Luminol. After that, I have no idea. There are a lot of things that react with Luminol. Maybe the floor lights up, maybe it doesn't.

So maybe the Luminol lit up in Steven Avery's garage because he used bleach to clean up blood on the floor or maybe it picked up on something else. Either way, I don't understand how he managed to shoot Teresa in the garage multiple times without making a giant bloody mess. It was a cluttered garage and clutter has a way of catching blood spatter. If she were standing when she was shot in the head, the blood spatter would have originated five-and-a-half feet off the ground and high-velocity spatter should have traveled all over the clutter. So I don't think she was standing up when she was shot. And I'm not entirely convinced she was conscious at the time, if alive at all.

Back to Teresa in Steven Avery's trailer. If she was shot in the garage, then what happened between the trailer and the garage? Obviously Avery could have been waiting with the rifle and walked her into the garage at gunpoint. That would explain why there was no sign of a big bloody struggle in the trailer. But we agreed earlier that this was a sexually motivated crime. What would he get out of it by walking her out to the garage and shooting her?

They found a set of shackles in Avery's house when they searched it. They were kinky shackles and he claimed that he purchased them to spice things up with his girlfriend. I would have thought that sex with a portly middle-aged felon would have been all of the spice a woman could ask for, but I guess I'm a prude. At any rate, Avery could have met Teresa at the door with the rifle and ordered her into the shackles. Teresa's DNA wasn't found on the shackles, but maybe Avery was the type of gentleman to clean his sex toys between uses.

The theory that I keep coming back to, even if I can't fully articulate why, is that Avery strangled her. I hate the theory because it would have been a painful and terrifying way for Teresa to die. I'd feel better knowing that Avery lured her out to the garage with some clever ruse and that she died instantly and painlessly from a gunshot to the head that she never saw coming. But I have this gut feeling that the sick son of a bitch strangled her to death. Let me outline it for you and see what you think.

During his interview with police, Steven Avery was adamant that Teresa never came in to his house. That is a bold claim to make if it wasn't true. Police recognized the opportunity to catch him in a lie and tried to scare him off that story. There is so much trace evidence that could be left behind when a person is in a house. Police laid out how hairs, fibers, fingerprints and DNA evidence works and Avery had to have recognized what it would mean if they found anything linking Halbach to his trailer. It would have been so easy for Avery to just say that she stepped in the trailer for a minute to collect his money or leave a receipt. Then he would have had an excuse if they found any traces of her in the trailer. But he didn't waiver. He insisted she was never in there. Maybe he was bluffing because he was that confident in how well he cleaned the place. But I think he was telling the truth. I don't think Teresa was in there.

Avery said he followed Teresa out to her car to give her the money for the photo shoot. He described talking with her at the driver's side door. This would have been in plain view of anybody who was passing by on the roadway or looking out the window of his sister's house. It would have been too risky for him to walk out there holding a rifle.

He could have knocked her unconscious by smashing her over the head with something, then thrown her in the back of her own car. But that would have also made a bloody mess. There was a small amount of Teresa's blood and hair in the rear of her car, but not consistent with having her head split open from a crushing blow.

I think Avery strangled Teresa at the door of her car, either with his hands or with some sort of makeshift ligature. He could have done it quickly and would have been mostly concealed from view by the vehicle. When he was done, he could have thrown her into the rear of her car and moved the car into his garage. If she nicked her head on something during the struggle or while he was moving her, it could have opened up a minor cut that would have left a small amount of blood and hair in the back of the car.

Once in the garage, Steven Avery could have acted on his sexual intentions while Teresa was bound, unconscious or already dead. I don't care to speculate on what Steven Avery did here. I'm going to think happy thoughts about what prison is like for murderers and skip to the end.

Like a million other guys in the midwest, Avery was a deer hunter. As such, he had undoubtedly used his garage to dress a dead deer before. From experience, he surely knew that he could make clean up easier and prevent a bloody mess by strategically placing plastic or newspaper and putting Teresa in a convenient spot before shooting her. And if she was already dead from the initial strangulation (which is the theory I choose to believe because there is less torture and suffering involved), then the gunshots would have produced minimal blood loss anyway.

"Why would he shoot her if she was already dead?" you ask. I refer you back to my earlier analysis: Weird people do weird stuff sometimes and we won't always know why. Or you can go with the alternate theory that she didn't die until he shot her, but I'm writing this so I am going with the lesser of two horrors.

From that point, it's pretty straightforward. Over the next two days he hid her vehicle in the salvage yard, hoping it wouldn't be found before he had a chance to do something more permanent, and burned her body and all of the evidence in the burn pit and burn barrels around his house. He didn't use the car crusher or the incinerator because he rarely used either of those things in the course of his job and didn't want his brother and father asking questions like "What car are you crushing?" or "What the hell are you burning in that incinerator?" while he was at the center of a missing person investigation. Eventually the plot was discovered, and Dean Strang became an unlikely heartthrob through Netflix.

OK, OK, stop screaming at me. We'll talk about Brendan Dassey. This was a terrible story to begin with, and it isn't going to get any better if we bring Brendan Dassey into it. But since you insist, here it is.

Brendan Dassey confessed to assisting his uncle Steven Avery with the rape, murder and disposal of Teresa Halbach. He was convicted. That conviction was overturned. Then it was upheld. Then depending on the day of the week, he is either free pending an appeal or back in jail.

Dassey told a story that was, according to the prosecutor, so rich in detail that it could not possibly have been made up. Dassey only could have gotten those details from being involved. In the professional opinion of old Barney Doyle, the confession is absolutely made up and the details Brendan Dassey gave don't match the crime scene at all. But what do I know? I wasn't there for the investigation and, even if I was, we have already established that I am a moron. Maybe he did do it after all.

Brendan was 16 years old at the time of the murder and lived with his mother and brothers next door to Steven Avery. Like everybody else in his family, Brendan was interviewed by police several days after the murder. He gave a story that was complete and utter horseshit, which put him on the police radar. His initial story was that he didn't see Teresa at the Avery Salvage Yard, but then he might have seen her, but then he definitely saw her leaving and driving away. Police rightfully suspected that Steven Avery had coached Brendan on what to tell them, and the details of his story crumbled under the slightest bit of scrutiny.

Several months later, police did a follow up interview with Brendan at his school. This time Brendan said that he saw Teresa's body in the burn pit behind Steven Avery's house on Halloween night while Avery was having a bonfire. He said that he was scared of Steven and didn't want to get him in trouble, so he didn't say anything.

The police came back and interviewed Brendan two more times. In those interviews, Brendan claimed that he actually first saw Teresa tied to Steven Avery's bed. Avery told Brendan to rape Teresa, which he did, then Steven slit Teresa's throat. They loaded her body into her car, for some unknown reason, and then burned her in the burn pit.

This was the story that got him convicted and I don't understand how. I will grant the prosecutor that it was rich in detail, but the details seem like nonsense to me. If Steven Avery slit Teresa's throat on his bed then there would have been blood all over that room. Blood would have absolutely soaked into the mattress. The prosecutor argued that Avery burned the sheets, and that was apparently good enough. Also, while Teresa's car was supposedly in the garage, why in the hell would they put her body in it? It's not like they drove her fifteen feet to the burn pit. And there was only a small amount of blood in the back of her car. If she had had her throat slit there would have been a lot of blood leading all the way from the bedroom to the car, and there is no way Avery could have cleaned that up well enough to hide it from the crime scene technicians.

I was working on a cold case homicide a few years ago where two men were wrongly convicted in the 1990s. A key piece of evidence was the testimony of a supposed co-conspirator, who was mentally challenged. While I was reviewing the transcripts of his police interview, I was struck by how completely off the guy's story was. He didn't get a single detail right that the investigators didn't tell him first. I met the investigators and knew them to be good men. I also knew that they firmly believed they had the right guys, right up until DNA proved otherwise. It's a really bad feeling when you aren't making progress in a murder case. It gets downright desperate if the case is high profile. Put enough pressure on an investigator and they will start to see things that aren't there and find meaning in things where there is none. I know why they believed what that guy was telling them, but with the benefit of time and distance it was clearly garbage.

I say that because I got a very similar sense reading the transcripts of Brendan Dassey's interviews. While I don't believe Dassey was as slow as his defense attorneys alleged, he was a sixteen year old kid and not a particularly smart one. He was a textbook candidate for a false confession. As I read his confession, I was troubled by how much of his story was either wrong or common knowledge. It seemed like the only time he got things "right" was when he was agreeing with statements that the investigators made.

Police were right to make him a suspect because he was clearly lying on the initial interview. I actually believed most of the second interview, when he described seeing the body in the fire. It was logical, it didn't contradict the known facts in any meaningful way, and it seemed like he was providing the information not agreeing to it. But I don't believe the rest of his confession and I certainly don't think it was believable enough to sustain a criminal conviction.

Plus, his confession contradicts our strangling theory and we have entirely too much invested in that to give up now.

That's not a bad start huh? We believe Steven Avery killed Teresa Halbach, acting alone. We have concerns about the integrity of some of the evidence, but ultimately not enough to come to a different conclusion. We think he attacked her in the driveway near her car and shot her in the garage, without ever taking her into his home. I think she was strangled and shot, but you aren't certain if you agree with that or not. We think Brendan Dassey learned about the crime after the fact, possibly seeing Teresa's body in Avery's burn pit, but that he loved and/or feared his uncle too much to say anything initially. We would hire Dean Strang and Jerome Buting if we were ever accused of murder. And this book would be a thousand times better if it were written by Kathleen Zellner.

I hope all of our cases go this smoothly.

The Murder of JonBenét Ramsey

I have a serious fear that one of my old cases will become famous one day. It terrifies me. I fear documentarians like rational people fear sharks or bears. I shudder at the opening credits to Dateline. I read newspapers with one hand over my eyes, praying that I don't recognize any familiar names beside the words "Innocence Project" or "newly discovered evidence."

I feel like I have been an above-average criminal investigator throughout my career and that I've done respectable work. But police never come off looking good in famous murders, and I'm sure more than one detective believed they were performing respectable work at the time only to hear otherwise from a narrative voiceover on a 13-part documentary years later.

There are a lot of opportunities to make minor errors and to do things imperfectly over the course of a complex criminal investigation. Nobody is flawless in any line of work, especially law enforcement. Most errors are minor and it is rare that any single error is large enough to ruin an entire investigation. But I still don't relish the idea of having my work scrutinized by the true crime community. "Who is this Doyle character and why is he photographing the victim's vehicle from that angle?" "Is this dope really going to collect the fired cartridge cases before he swabs the blood stains?" "Is it normal for the interrogator to sweat so much in an interview? This guy needs to lose some weight."

Who needs that in their life?

Because of this fear, I am reluctant to criticize the investigative decisions in most of these cases. The people on the ground are processing a lot of information very quickly and are making the best decisions they can. Most of them are probably smarter than me anyway, and if they made mistakes you can be pretty sure that old Barney Doyle probably would have made a few too.

With that in mind, I will reluctantly say that there is no way to defend the Boulder Police Department's initial response to the disappearance of JonBenét Ramsey. It doesn't resemble anything any police department should ever do in a similar situation and it doomed the investigation so completely that the case will likely never be solved.

But we'll get to that later. For now, let's talk about JonBenét.

JonBenét Ramsey was a six-year-old girl from a wealthy family living in Boulder Colorado. She lived with her parents, John and Patsy, and her nine-year-old brother Burke. Her father also had three children from a previous marriage. Two were grown and lived in Atlanta. A third was killed in a car crash before JonBenét was born.

I won't go into too much detail about what JonBenét was like because I have no idea. I don't know what her hopes and dreams were. I don't know what her fears were. I don't know anything about her. She was six years old. I know what other people have written about her, but I put very little stock in that. She was an adorable six-year-old kid. Like all kids that age she was just starting a life of limitless potential. That's the tragedy of a child murder. But not for the actions of some monster, JonBenét would have become something in life. We don't know what that something was, and now nobody ever will.

We've been hit over the head with her beauty pageant "career" since the day this story broke. I don't understand that world, but it exists. It seems like a cesspool of pedophiles and weirdos to me, but that's from the outside looking in. Maybe it's not that at all. I do wish the first line of every JonBenét story didn't mention the pageants though. I don't know what she would have done with her life, but I'm confident it would have involved more than a tiara and a sash.

I also know that when we started this mission we said we were going to solve some murders. And solving this one would be big for us. We'd be celebrated throughout the land for bringing justice for JonBenét. But it won't happen this time. This one isn't going to be solved with the information we have. We'll do our best to read the evidence and form a few theories. We'll calculate some odds and put forth some probabilities. But we can't be certain about any of it. This evidence just doesn't allow for it. It's too ambiguous, too contaminated and too thin.

That's not to say this is, as the CBS miniseries title implied, a *Perfect Murder, Perfect Town*. Boulder is a fine town. This was a tragedy of a murder, done sloppily by a monster of a human being. I doubt this case will ever be solved by way of a criminal conviction, but it would be giving the perpetrator way too much credit to imply that it was craftily committed. This murder was not particularly complex. It looks that way now, in much the same way that a child's jigsaw puzzle would look complex if you ran the pieces through a paper shredder first. The killer almost certainly left more than enough evidence to get caught, the police just failed to protect and collect that evidence before it was lost forever.

The Boulder District Attorney's Office immediately got cozy with a team of lawyers hired by the Ramseys despite the fact that the Ramseys were the primary suspects at the time. It led to a bitter feud between the police and the prosecutors that made a bad investigation worse. It's not necessarily the District Attorney's job to investigate crimes, but it certainly isn't their place to hinder a criminal investigation either. From the outside looking in, it sure seemed like they were more of an obstacle than an aid.

And while we are throwing out some blame, the legal team hired by the Ramseys either did an unconscionable disservice to their clients or they performed miracles, depending on which theory you believe. If nobody in the Ramsey family participated in JonBenét's murder then John Ramsey should hate his attorneys as much as he hates the actual murderer. He and his family could have been cleared of suspicion within the first day or two and police could have turned all of their resources toward finding the killer. Since both sides would have been working toward the same goal, a war between the District Attorney's office and the Boulder Police Department probably wouldn't have happened and there was a reasonable chance that the case could have been solved while the trail was still fresh. By fleeing the area and surrounding themselves with lawyers and avoiding the police and parading in front of the media—all surely at the direction of their attorneys— the Ramseys gave the same impression to the police that they gave to everybody else in the world: the Ramseys were guilty as sin. The police wasted months trying to build a case against the Ramseys while all hope of catching the actual killer dissipated into the air. That is not what an innocent person pays an attorney for.

If, however, somebody in the Ramsey family was the real killer, John Ramsey owes the world to those attorneys. As shitty and infuriating as the Ramseys' actions were in the months following the murder, nobody from that household is ever going to prison for JonBenét's murder. And that is ultimately what a guilty person pays an attorney for.

There are a million articles, books, television shows, mini-series and documentaries about this crime. They mostly have the same information, but everybody puts their own little spin on things. Not us. No spin for us. We are strictly about the facts around here. And our deductions, of course, but those are better than everybody else's deductions.

For our purposes, we are taking our facts from former Boulder Police Detective Steve Thomas' book *JonBenét: Inside the Ramsey Murder Investigation*, *Listen Carefully: Truth and Evidence in the JonBenét Ramsey Case* from True Crimes Detective Guild, *The Cases that Haunt Us* by John Douglas and Mark Olshaker, and press coverage from the Boulder Daily Camera and the Denver Post.

On December 26, 1996, at 5:52 a.m., Patsy Ramsey called 911 to report that her six-year-old daughter, JonBenét, had been kidnapped. She told the dispatcher that she had found a ransom note on the staircase and discovered her daughter was missing.

Boulder police responded immediately and did a thorough and professional job of processing the crime scene. Wait a second, let me check my notes. Scratch that, they did the opposite. They did a half-assed and unprofessional job of bungling the crime scene.

John, Patsy and Burke Ramsey were all home at the time of the 911 call. Several uniformed officers, detectives and crime scene investigators responded to the scene to begin the investigation. In a perfect world, officers would have taken the Ramseys away from the home so that they could get separate statements from each of them while crime scene technicians carefully searched the house for evidence. The Ramsey phone line would have been forwarded to the police station and monitored so that any communication with the kidnapper could be intercepted. In a less than ideal world, the officers would have done the same thing but perhaps while allowing one of the Ramseys to remain in the home to respond to any communication from the kidnappers. In Boulder on that morning, officers not only failed to search the house but also allowed the Ramseys to invite a half-dozen friends over to defile the crime scene.

This is usually the place in the story where somebody defends the Boulder Police Department by saying that they did not know they were investigating a murder right away. Fair point. They believed they were investigating a home-invasion child abduction. A home-invasion child abduction is about the only crime I can think of that warrants a more serious response than a homicide. The way the police handled the crime scene would have been improper for a dognapping. It was unforgivable for a reported kidnapping.

Initial responding officers checked around the house but did not observe any obvious signs of a break-in. Rumors circulated later that there was snow around the house and that there were no shoe impressions in the snow leading to any of the windows. Photographs showed that most of the backyard, particularly around the windows, had no snow. Boulder Police Chief Mark Beckner claimed there was a layer of frost on the ground and that officers did not see shoe impressions in the frost. It does not appear that crime scene photos were taken in time to corroborate that observation, so we are left at the mercy of the memories and descriptions of the responding officers.

Officers took John Ramsey with them on a cursory walk-through of the house. Not to beat a dead horse here, but if for some reason you and I ever find ourselves processing a crime scene together, we will not be doing that. At any rate, they did not observe any sign of a struggle in JonBenét's room.

John and Patsy Ramsey gave initial statements to the police in which they said that they last saw JonBenét when they placed her in bed the previous night. The Ramseys were at a Christmas party and JonBenét had fallen asleep in the car on the ride home. John said that he carried JonBenét to her room, still asleep, and placed her in bed. Patsy said that she changed JonBenét's shirt and tucked her in. John claimed that the investigators misunderstood what he said, and the truth was he read in his bed after putting JonBenét in her own bed.

Investigators found the ransom note on the floor and were confused to learn that it was three pages long. I've never worked a kidnapping case with a ransom note so I don't know how long they are supposed to be, but three pages seems excessive. Notes in most bank robberies can fit on a napkin. The criminal is just trying to extort money, not publish a thesis.

The initial responding officers said they found the note on the floor where John Ramsey said he saw it. Crime scene photographs actually showed the note on the staircase where Patsy Ramsey said she discovered it. Don't read anything into the discrepancy. I'm sure the investigators placed it there to show where Patsy found it, even though staging evidence is something officers are really encouraged not to do. You could fill a book with errors made on this crime scene. Several people already have. We're doing a pretty good job of it ourselves, come to think of it.

The note was odd. It was written on a notepad from the Ramseys' kitchen and we'll discuss the handwriting later. But even the words themselves are odd. I won't do it justice describing it, so I'll let you read it in its entirety and see what you think:

Mr. Ramsey,

Listen carefully! We are a group of individuals that represent a small foreign faction. We respect your bussiness [sic] but not the country that it serves. At this time we have your daughter in our posession [sic]. She is safe and unharmed and if you want her to see 1997 you must follow our instructions to the letter.

You will withdraw $118,000.00 from your account. $100,000 will be in $100 bills and the remaining $18,000 in $20 bills. Make sure that you bring an adequate size attache to the bank. When you get home you will put the money in a brown paper bag. I will call you between 8 and 10 am tomorrow to instruct you on delivery. The delivery will be exhausting so I advise you to be rested. If we monitor you getting the money early, we might call you early to arrange an earlier delivery of the money and hence a earlier pick-up of your daughter.

Any deviation of my instructions will result in the immediate execution of your daughter. You will also be denied her remains for proper burial. The two gentlemen watching over your daughter do not particularly like you so I advise you not to provoke them. Speaking to anyone about your situation, such as Police, F.B.I., etc., will result in your daughter being beheaded. If we catch you talking to a stray dog, she dies. If you alert bank authorities, she dies. If the money is in any way marked or tampered with, she dies. You will be scanned for electronic devices and if any are found, she dies. You can try to deceive us, but be warned that we are familiar with Law enforcement countermeasures and tactics. You stand a 99% chance of killing your daughter if you try to out smart us. Follow our instructions and you stand a 100% chance of getting her back. You and your family are under constant scrutiny as well as the authorities. Don't try to grow a brain John. You are not the only fat cat around so don't think that killing will be difficult. Don't underestimate us John. Use that good southern common sense of yours. It is up to you now John!

Victory!

S.B.T.C

What do you think? Weird right? That was a pain in my ass to type out, I can't imagine what it was like to think of and handwrite. And what the hell is with the delivery instructions? An attache? An exhausting delivery? Familiar with police countermeasures? Two more pages of that and it would have been the script for another *Die Hard* movie.

Several professional document examiners and several thousand amateurs have examined the letter and determined that the handwriting has some similarities to

Patsy Ramsey's. I know you are skeptical of handwriting analysis and you should be. It isn't an exact science and don't ever believe a document examiner who claims it is. Plus, the term "handwriting analysis" gets thrown around by people who are doing drastically different things. Most of us think of handwriting analysis as a comparison of the structure of handwritten letters, numbers and symbols to look for similarities and differences between documents with an unknown author and samples with a known author. That's reasonable. Intuitively it seems like there should be noticeable differences between different people's handwriting. Other people use the term "handwriting analysis" to describe a discipline where people determine personality traits about the author based on handwriting. Like astrology, but with penmanship. That's not reasonable. Not for our purposes anyway.

There is also an approach called linguistic analysis and another one referred to as statement analysis. Linguistic analysis compares the vocabulary and word choices used in a questioned document to that of a known suspect. Statement analysis examines a document to look for signs of deception. Both are interesting approaches that still need more research. I would certainly consider either approach as valid in terms of identifying potential investigative avenues, but I wouldn't consider the results of either analysis to be evidence. They just aren't consistent enough.

So while there are "handwriting experts" out there who have publicly proclaimed that the ransom letter was definitely written by Patsy Ramsey, I'm not comfortable going that far. I haven't heard of a single expert who determined that Patsy Ramsey was absolutely not the author, but I also haven't read anything to convince me that she absolutely was. Let's just accept that her handwriting shares some similarities, and work from there.

Police had been at the Ramsey house for a couple of hours before Burke Ramsey got out of bed. In an interview with TV's Dr. Phil two decades later, Burke said that he was awake in bed but didn't come downstairs because he was afraid and didn't know what was going on. A family friend, Fleet White, eventually got Burke out of bed to take him to Fleet's home so that Burke wouldn't have to be around the scene. An officer tried to talk with Burke before he left to find out if Burke knew anything. John would not allow the officer to talk to Burke. John claimed that Burke had been asleep and did not know anything. John Ramsey made a lot of decisions over the course of the investigation that made him look like he was hiding things. Maybe there were innocent reasons behind all of his actions, but it's not hard to see why so many casual observers doubted him.

There was no call from the kidnappers by 10:00 a.m., and apparently everybody in the Boulder Police Department had better things to do than work the scene of a home-invasion child abduction. A single detective was left at the home with the Ramseys, four family friends and a pastor. That detective couldn't keep track of all of those people, so folks wandered unsupervised throughout the crime scene while she tried, without success, to summon additional officers.

At a little before 1:00 p.m., the detective sent John Ramsey and Fleet White to go search the house for clues. Ideally you would rather have a law enforcement officer search the crime scene for clues instead of two people who would eventually be investigated as suspects, but I guess you work with what you have.

Ramsey and White found JonBenét's body in a room in the basement. According to both of them, it was John Ramsey who found her. She was already dead, her mouth covered with a piece of black tape and her wrists bound with nylon cord. There was also a nylon cord garrote around her neck with what appeared to be a broken paint brush handle used for tension. She was clothed in what she had worn to bed, but covered with a blanket, and there was a pink nightgown beside her. Her hands were stretched out over her head. This was all based on descriptions by Ramsey and White, however, because Ramsey carried JonBenét's body upstairs before photographs could be taken or the scene could be processed.

OK, we'll talk about it now. I know you've researched this before and remember there being some controversy about what JonBenét wore to bed. Patsy Ramsey seems to have given inconsistent statements about what JonBenét was wearing. Some folks call those inconsistent statements evidence that Patsy participated in the killing. We are better than that. If you and I are investigating a murder and our prime suspect tells us that he was at the roller disco with his grandma during the murder but then tells us later that he was actually at the adult theater with a guy from work, we'll make note of those inconsistent statements. Where he was at and who he was with at the time of the murder are very relevant to the investigation and a person doesn't easily forget a night at the roller disco or the porno theater (I would imagine). But if he claims to have had French fries with his dinner but later says it was cole slaw, we don't really care. That probably isn't important to the investigation and a reasonable person wouldn't be expected to remember it anyway. Point being, there are a lot of very valid reasons why we have our suspicions about Patsy Ramsey, but we aren't going to cheapen those reasons with nonsense like this. JonBenét's pajamas have no real significance to this investigation and a reasonable person probably wouldn't remember a detail like that anyway.

The room where JonBenét was found was commonly referred to as a wine cellar in most of the coverage of the crime. It was mainly just a storage area, but there were ground-level exterior windows in the room. Several officers and witnesses claimed that they had seen the door closed and latched that morning. White had looked in the room briefly at some point but it was too dark for him to see JonBenét's body. None of the officers looked in the room, however, because they believed that since the door latched from the outside that there was no way the kidnapper could have escaped that way.

I can't imagine the shock of the poor detective who saw John Ramsey carrying JonBenét's body into the sitting room. She made a couple of panicked 911 calls to summon help from the other officers who were out doing God knows what while she was alone in an uncontrollable crime scene. While she was getting help, everybody else in the house contaminated either the body or the location she was found. Some managed to do both. None of it was malicious, just people reacting to a tragedy. But the scene was so thoroughly contaminated that if any of the people in the house that day did commit the murder there would be no way that trace evidence from JonBenét or the scene could be used against them.

The Ramsey family was supposed to fly to Michigan that morning. After discovering the body, John Ramsey changed plans and decided the family should go to their other home in Georgia. Friends and investigating officers had to convince John that it was poor form to leave the state in the middle of his daughter's murder investigation, particularly when he was a either a crucial witness or a prime suspect. Then he surrounded himself in lawyers and provided the police with no meaningful assistance toward finding his daughter's killer. I can hear your teeth grinding from here. Yes, it was shitty. Yes, it makes him look guilty as hell.

In John Ramsey's defense, the police believed early on that he was involved in the murder and most people would be reluctant to help the police put them in prison. In the police's defense, most people watching from the outside believed John Ramsey had something to do with the murder, too. In defense of those people, he might have had something to do with the murder. But it's really hard to judge guilt or innocence based off of how people react to their daughter's murder and the resulting intrusive media coverage, so let's get back to the actual evidence.

The medical examiner got to the Ramsey house at about 8:00 p.m. for a preliminary examination. He noted that JonBenét's arms were still extended over her head. She had a ligature around her neck and another around her right wrist. There was also a small bruise on her right cheek below the ear.

During the autopsy, the medical examiner noted that the ligature on the right wrist was tied loosely and over the sleeve of her long-sleeve shirt. It was a white nylon cord and there was a double-loop at the other end, 15½ inches from the right wrist. For reference sake, the chain on my handcuffs is 2 inches long. And I keep another set of hinged handcuffs with no chain because 2 inches can be too much slack sometimes. JonBenét's hands may have been tied together, but not in a way that would have restrained her in any meaningful way.

JonBenét was wearing a set of long underwear over regular underwear. There was some red staining on the crotch. There was also dried blood on her vagina. And yes, it was as uncomfortable for me to type that as it was for you to read it. So uncomfortable that I'm not going into the specific injuries that led to this conclusion. Let's just say that the consensus among several medical examiners was that JonBenét had been molested, but that the assailant did not have sexual intercourse with her. The experts also determined that there was trauma consistent with chronic sexual abuse over a period of time, not just a one-time assault from her killer.

There was petechial hemorrhaging, which are little pinpoint dots that commonly show up in stranglings, on JonBenét's eyelids. The ligature around her neck appeared to be the same white cord that was around her wrists. What appeared to be a broken paint brush handle was used to tighten the ligature.

There was livor mortis on her back and the right side of the face. Livor mortis is a purplish color that appears where the blood settles after it stops pumping. It gives you an idea of the position the body was in after the death. In this case, she was on her back with her head turned to the right side.

There were marks on JonBenét's back and the side of her face that certain investigators claimed were consistent with injuries from a stun gun. The claim is dubious, but we'll at least mention it.

JonBenét's stomach had nothing in it but pineapple. A bowl of pineapple was found on the Ramseys' kitchen table. File this away because it will matter later.

It wasn't visible on the external examination, but the medical examiner found a large scalp hemorrhage and accompanying fracture on JonBenét's skull. The medical examiners determined that the injury to the head happened before the strangulation, although either would have been fatal on their own.

OK, that wasn't fun. Sorry. That poor little girl. Take a break if you need to. I'm going to grab a beer real quick before we move on.

[beer break]

OK, let's get back to business. We wouldn't have gone into all of those gory details if we didn't need to. I'm proud of you for getting through it. We couldn't make guesses about who killed JonBenét without knowing at least that much. We may not figure out for certain who killed JonBenét, but we can say for absolute damn sure that the person was human garbage. So let's start sniffing around and try to figure out who that garbage might have been.

As we discussed before, there was quite a pissing match between the prosecutors and the police on this one. The cops said that the Ramseys had to have done it, specifically Patsy Ramsey. The prosecutors, at least initially, were pushing hard to look for an intruder. I feel confident that it was either somebody who lived in the Ramsey house or somebody who didn't. And also that they were alive in 1996. I'll step out on that limb too. The rest is going to be pure speculation.

Let's examine the competing theories in light of what we know.

John Ramsey

The facts that point to John Ramsey:

The single most damning thing I can think of going against John Ramsey is his lack of cooperation at the start of the investigation. It was the murder of his daughter. I give people all kinds of leeway when it comes to how they react to a tragedy like that. Some will be extremely emotional. Some will be weirdly stoic. Some will go into obvious shock and others will look like they are barely affected at all. But regardless of their outward appearance, I would expect any innocent parent to move heaven and earth to help the police find the killer of their child. Ramsey moved heaven and earth to give the appearance that he was helping the police find the killer of his daughter, mostly through television interviews, but actually just ducked behind layers of lawyers and excuses until police were certain he was involved with the murder.

The medical examiners also believed that JonBenét suffered through a history of sexual molestation. In most cases where a child is molested by an unknown person, the first suspect is usually the father or the stepfather. If John was molesting JonBenét, the odds of him committing a sexually-motivated murder go up drastically.

Police did not find any sign of forced entry at the Ramsey home, and John allegedly told police that he had checked the doors and windows prior to going to bed that night. Of the people in the home, John Ramsey is the closest in age and gender to the suspect you would expect to find in a sexually-motivated homicide. John also claimed to have carried JonBenét from the car to her bed when they returned from the Christmas party, making him one of the last known people to have seen JonBenét alive. Burke contradicted John in a later interview and said that he remembered JonBenét being awake when they returned home and walking up the stairs on her own.

A neighbor told police that she heard a loud scream coming from the direction of the Ramsey home at about

2:00 a.m. on the morning JonBenét was found. If a neighbor could hear it, in December in Colorado when all of the windows were closed, then how could the family in the home not hear it? Again, if somebody who lived in the home committed the murder, statistics would point to John.

There was no sign of a struggle in JonBenét's bedroom. Either she was soundly asleep, incapable of fighting back, or went with her killer willingly. Logically, you would think she would go willingly with her father.

John Ramsey discovered JonBenét's body when the on-scene detective told him to go search the home for clues. According to Fleet White, who went with him, John Ramsey went directly to the basement where JonBenét was found. Also according to White, John Ramsey saw JonBenét immediately from the doorway. White had already looked in the room earlier that morning and claimed he couldn't see JonBenét from the doorway.

JonBenét was also covered by a blanket with her favorite nightgown beside her. Those types of delicate touches are commonly associated with a killer who, perversely, cared about the victim and felt remorse for the act. John Ramsey obviously loved JonBenét and would have undoubtedly felt guilty if he killed her.

And as the living embodiment of every stereotype about wealthy white men, John Ramsey was into sailboats. Of course he was. Which meant that he was obviously familiar with knots. And probably white khakis, but that's unrelated to what we are working on here.

John and Patsy both gave vague and sometimes inconsistent accounts of what exactly happened after Patsy found the ransom note. Most of the inconsistencies had to do with where John was in the house when Patsy discovered the note, and when they checked on Burke. In one account, John claimed to have checked the entire house and gotten dressed in between the time Patsy called 911 and when the police arrived. Obviously he didn't check the entire house or he would have found JonBenét, and it was only four minutes between the 911 call and the first officer's arrival. Under stress, it would take me that long to get my underwear on in the right direction.

The facts that point away from John Ramsey:

John was never accused of molesting his or any other children either prior to or after JonBenét's death. That's not the kind of thing a person starts doing in their 40s. There is usually a pattern of behavior, especially if it escalates all the way to murder. Now, I understand that John was rich and that rich people have more resources to hide devious details of their lives, but there was so much police scrutiny in this case. And that's saying nothing about the tabloid journalists digging into every sordid detail. I cannot believe John could have molested children without it coming to light at some point.

Similarly, John Ramsey had no history of violence. It's pretty unprecedented for a person's first act of violence to be a sexual homicide of their own six-year-old daughter.

Police conducted some unscientific experiments in the Ramsey home several months after the murder and determined that it was possible for the neighbor to hear something from the basement of the home that might not be heard from John and Patsy's bedroom.

The body was found in the Ramsey home. If John had killed JonBenét and concocted the ransom story as a cover, why would he have disposed of the body in the home? And why would John have "discovered" the body if he had killed her? The police were buying the kidnapping story and it was working in his favor. Finding the body in the home predictably made him a prime suspect. Obviously he could not have planned for police incompetence, but wouldn't John have done more to exploit it if he were the killer?

Patsy Ramsey

The facts that point to Patsy Ramsey:

The ransom note is the big one. They got handwriting from a lot of people in this investigation and Patsy's writing sure seemed to be the closest to a match. And it was written on a tablet and with a pen from the Ramsey kitchen. Plus there were indentations on the tablet from what appeared to be a rough draft of the ransom letter. It was Patsy's paper, Patsy's pen and possibly Patsy's handwriting.

The note also demanded $118,000 in ransom. As it happened, John had just gotten a Christmas bonus for that exact amount.

When police arrived on the morning of the murder, Patsy was wearing the same outfit that she had worn to the party the night before and was in full makeup. As mentioned before, there were only four minutes between her 911 call and the arrival of the first officer. So when did she get ready? Maybe it was before she went downstairs and discovered the note. Or maybe she was up the entire night participating in a murder and cover-up.

Patsy was hysterical while speaking to the 911 operator, but the phone call did not disconnect right away when Patsy hung up the phone and the operator believed Patsy's demeanor calmed immediately after Patsy believed the call disconnected, suggesting that the hysterics may have been an act.

There was pineapple found in JonBenét's stomach during the autopsy and a bowl of pineapple was on the Ramsey's kitchen table when police arrived. But Patsy insisted that JonBenét was asleep when they got home from the party and therefore could not have eaten the pineapple. If Patsy was lying about such a seemingly insignificant detail there must have been a reason, right? Why did she not want investigators to think that JonBenét was awake when they got home?

Patsy was also a former beauty pageant contestant and, depending on who you believe, may have been the driving force behind JonBenét's pageant participation. Some of the books and media coverage have painted her as an overbearing mother who expected perfection from JonBenét.

The facts that point away from Patsy Ramsey:

Nobody has ever credibly accused Patsy of molesting JonBenét or any other child. She also doesn't have a documented history of violence. JonBenét's murder would have been unbelievably brutal for a person's first crime, particularly for a woman. Not to be sexist against female murderers, but they just don't usually start with the brutal sexual murder of their own child.

Patsy was wearing the same clothes that she had worn to the party the night before, but they didn't have any blood on them. In addition to the blood on JonBenét's underwear, investigators also found evidence that blood had been wiped up from JonBenét's legs. It's tough to commit a hands-on murder and keep your clothes clean. I can't eat a hands-on cheeseburger without leaving evidence on my shirt.

Patsy was undergoing treatment for ovarian cancer in 1996. You can see in her television interviews that she seemed fatigued, medicated and meek. She might have been playing it up. And it wouldn't take an Olympic weightlifter to overpower JonBenét. But it's still kind of hard to envision Patsy having the physical stamina to commit such a murder.

There are a lot of people who say Patsy wasn't the killer but that she orchestrated the cover-up. The implication there is that John or Burke killed JonBenét. This would mean that Patsy cared more about one child than the other, or more about her husband than her daughter, or more about her husband's fortune than her daughter's life.

I'm pretty cynical, but I don't know if I'm that cynical. You might be, but you're wiser about the world than I am. I won't pretend to know what Patsy Ramsey was really like, but she'd have to be a real monster in this scenario. Maybe she was, but I would like some more evidence before I go to that conclusion.

Similarly, there are quite a few people suggesting that Patsy Ramsey accidentally killed JonBenét in a fit of rage because JonBenét wet her bed. I hope that seems as absurd to you as it does to me. I understand that toileting issues can be stressful for parents and children. Hell, I still won't pretend that I've mastered all of the nuances of the human bladder. But sending a mother into a rage so violent that she accidentally kills her daughter? And then rather than seeking medical help she disguises the death as a sex crime? All from bedwetting? I just can't see it.

Burke Ramsey

The facts that point to Burke Ramsey:

Statistically speaking, most child murders are committed by a family member or close friend. Burke Ramsey was a family member.

Certain audio technicians swear that Burke Ramsey can be heard in the background of Patsy Ramsey's 911 call, but Patsy and John were adamant that he was in bed asleep at the time. Those technicians claim that Burke can be heard asking John and Patsy what they found and that John can be heard telling Burke that they weren't talking to him, or something to that effect.

Just a word of caution, audio enhancements are notoriously unreliable. In the absence of clearly audible speech, listeners tend to hear what they want to hear. I'm not telling you to disregard it if you think you can hear something on that recording, but I'm not putting much stock in the background chatter on the 911 calls. I've been burned too many times by audio enhancements.

The facts that point away from Burke Ramsey:

He was nine years old.

The first attention I really paid to this case was when I read the John Douglas book *The Cases That Haunt Us* in about 2001. John Douglas was one of the first FBI Agents assigned to the famed Behavioral Analysis Unit, a unit that we outsiders commonly refer to as "profilers." (He was the real-life Holden, if you've ever watched Mindhunter on Netflix.) I had read Douglas' other books where he talked about elements of modus operandi, signatures and staging. Everything he wrote before *The Cases That Haunt Us* would lead you to believe that a member of the Ramsey family killed JonBenét. In *The Cases That Haunt Us*, Douglas insisted that an intruder killed JonBenét. It's probably just a coincidence, but in the name of transparency I will mention that the Ramseys paid Douglas a sizable consultation fee to help prove that they didn't kill JonBenét.

I was so frustrated with Douglas when I read that book because he was so dismissive of the idea that Patsy or John Ramsey killed JonBenét. She was covered with a blanket. There was evidence of sexual abuse. She was carefully staged. Everything he wrote about in his previous books said it had to be a family member. Why was he forsaking me? Then it hit me: I wonder if JonBenét had a brother? A few paragraphs later Douglas casually mentions the existence of Burke Ramsey, but never mentioned him again. Aha! Burke Ramsey did it! Douglas wasn't lying to me about John and Patsy Ramsey, he just somehow missed Burke. I solved the case from two thousand miles away without ever visiting the crime scene. I was a genius!

I was 21 years old at the time. It had been a dozen years since I was a 9-year-old kid. I had no conception of what 9-year-olds were like. Now that I've been an adult for a while, especially as a police officer, I'm much more aware of what 9-year-olds are like. They are wild animals that can do basic math and ride bicycles. Some of them are assholes. They all cheat at video games. Some of them lie. Some of them steal. But virtually none of them commit murder.

I dug through the annals of Wikipedia to find a comparable murder that might prove Burke was a plausible suspect. I couldn't do it. An 8-year-old boy in India killed three infants by beating them to death with stones in about 2007. Two 10-year-old boys tortured and murdered a 3-year-old in England in 1993. But those victims were way younger than JonBenét. All of the other documented killers around Burke's age used firearms. Even those cases were extremely rare. And all of those kids seemed to have profound behavioral issues leading up to the killings.

Burke Ramsey had no significant behavioral issues that I'm aware of before or after JonBenét's death. He was only three years older than her and I've read nothing to suggest that he was some sort of savant with ligatures and garrotes. I'm not saying it is impossible that Burke Ramsey was the killer. But if he was, then this was the strangest damn case that I've ever heard of. And I don't think it was him.

Sorry 21-year-old Barney Doyle, I know how certain you were at the time.

An intruder

The facts that point to an intruder:

There was at least one ground-floor window found unsecured on the morning that JonBenét's body was discovered. The window was big enough for a grown man to crawl through and led to the basement.

There was a Hi-Tec brand boot impression on the floor near where JonBenét was found. The impression was never matched to anybody.

Police did not find any white cord in the Ramsey residence that matched the ligature found on JonBenét. Nor did they find any tape that matched what was found on JonBenét's mouth.

There were marks on JonBenét's back that certain experts attributed to a stun gun. There was no stun gun found in the Ramsey residence.

The DNA of an unknown male was discovered in JonBenét's underwear.

The facts that point away from an intruder:

Police insist that frost, light snow, vegetation and spiderwebs around the unsecured window were undisturbed on the morning JonBenét's body was found.

Police discovered a receipt from the local hardware store showing that the Ramseys made a purchase three weeks before the murder. The receipt didn't say what item was purchased, but it was for the exact same price as some white nylon cord that was similar to what was found on JonBenét.

In spite of what some people seem to think, JonBenét was not incapacitated by a stun gun. That's not how stun guns work. Back when old Barney Doyle was young Barney Doyle, working patrol shifts in a small town police department, he experienced and witnessed a fair amount of workplace shenanigans. Some involved an old-school stun gun that the chief had somehow acquired. It wasn't a Taser that police might legitimately use for work. It was the type of stun gun that 1980s women might use to fend off an attacker or sadistic police supervisors might use to torment patrol officers for cheap entertainment. That damn thing hurt and it scared the crap out of you, but it wasn't capable of incapacitating anybody, even a small child. To the contrary, it would wake you up if you happened to doze off at your desk on a slow shift.

The Ramsey house was huge and confusingly laid out. An intruder would have had a very difficult time navigating it in the dark, finding JonBenét's room and taking her to the basement without being detected.

The ransom note was written in the Ramsey's home. What kind of kidnapper would plan ahead enough to bring the ligature and the tape but not the ransom note?

Also, the DNA found in JonBenét's underwear was not from semen, blood or saliva. It was what is commonly referred to as touch DNA that can be transferred by handling an object. Patsy Ramsey said that the underwear was brand new out of the package, so that DNA could have been left by anybody in the manufacturing and packaging process. There is also some controversy as to whether the DNA found in JonBenét's underwear is from a single source or just a contaminated sample from multiple sources.

Which brings up an important point about DNA. There seems to be this belief among the general public that DNA evidence is some magic tool that can solve any crime. It's just evidence. It means nothing without context. Sometimes it can show that a specific person was in a specific location—much like a fingerprint. Other times it can show that a man ejaculated somewhere. Other times it can show that a person bled somewhere. Other times it can show that a person drooled somewhere. It can show a lot of different things, but they are all dependent on context. It is up to people like you and me to think critically about what the DNA means among all of the other details of an investigation.

Speaking of critical thinking, it's probably about time we came to our conclusion on this thing. I warned you it wasn't going to be easy. The answer isn't obvious on this one. But I can see from that look in your eye that you've got a pretty good guess. I think I do too. Let's say it together at the same time. Count of three. One. Two. Three!

Dang it. You said one of the Ramseys didn't you? I was afraid of that. You're probably right. You usually are. But I think it was an intruder. Let me lay out my theory for you, then we can agree to disagree and move on to something else

The statistics say that when a child JonBenét's age is murdered that it is usually the parents who did it. Usually, but not always. When a child JonBenét's age is murdered there is also usually a long history of child abuse. It usually involves a panicked trip to the emergency room and a convoluted story about an improbable "accident" and some pleading not to notify the police. Or it involves the complete disappearance of the child, followed several days later by the discovery of the body near the home and a pile of evidence pointing right to the parents. JonBenét was found in her home, sexually assaulted and with no prior reports of child abuse. It wasn't a usual murder.

And while molestation is tragically common within families, there is almost always a multi-generational pattern associated with it. There are murmurs around the family, weird dynamics and odd behavior. Sure, JonBenét wet the bed and that can be a symptom of sexual abuse. But there is a benign explanation for bedwetting more often than a sinister one, and when there is a sinister explanation there are usually a bunch of other red flags as well. I haven't found any evidence of widespread molestation within the Ramsey family.

But the medical examiners did find evidence that JonBenét had been molested. Not just on the night of the murder, but chronic molestation over a period of time. The suspect did not have sexual intercourse with JonBenét but did abuse her. That could be taken a couple of different ways. Either the person was savvy enough to realize that JonBenét would be injured by sexual intercourse and that they would be caught. Or they were sexually unsophisticated and incapable, for whatever reason, of sexual intercourse.

I downplayed JonBenét's participation in child beauty pageants earlier because I don't want her to be defined by an aspect of her life that I doubt she had much say in. I played T-ball at that age, but I'm sure it was more my parents' idea than it was mine. Of course T-ball isn't a cesspool of child exploitation and pedophilia. Draw your own conclusion about child beauty pageants.

I am extremely grateful that I have never been assigned to work crimes against children in my police career. I have a few friends who work in those units and it is heartbreaking. I've helped on the fringes of a few cases and learned more than I ever wanted to know. The world of pedophiles is something that most of us can't wrap our minds around. They are profoundly damaged human beings. They can speak openly among themselves on internet forums about raping toddlers while sincerely believing that they are doing nothing wrong. Many of them truly believe they are being persecuted by the rest of us. How can you argue right and wrong with somebody who doesn't instinctively know that it is wrong to rape a child?

But even if some of these people don't believe they are doing anything wrong, they do recognize that the rest of the world thinks they are wrong. So away from the anonymity of the internet, they hide that side of themselves as well as they can. Some are very successful at hiding. Police catch the others either molesting children or exchanging child pornography.

I think that it was a pedophile who killed JonBenét. I think he was obsessed with JonBenét and that he probably discovered her at one of those damned pageants. I think he convinced himself that he and JonBenét were in love and that, although there was nothing wrong with that love, he still had to hide it from everybody else. I think he ingratiated himself into some aspect of JonBenét's life (pageants, school, dance class, etc.) so that he could have access to her. I think he molested her, but either through flattery or gifts or threats convinced her not to tell anybody. And I think at some point he convinced himself that he and JonBenét should run away and be together.

Boulder in 1996 was not the type of place where people were overly concerned with home security. Anybody patient and determined enough to check a few windows and doors would have gotten into the Ramsey house eventually. I think JonBenét's killer got in there sometime Christmas Day while the Ramseys were away and hid in the basement until everybody went to bed.

I think the killer's "plan" was to run away with JonBenét. I don't think the killer was a mentally sophisticated person and I don't know that he'd worked out all of the details beforehand. He probably knew, on some level, that JonBenét might not run away with him and that he may have to resort to violence. So he brought the rope and tape, just in case.

I think that while he was waiting for the Ramseys to return from the Christmas Party, he decided that a fake ransom note would throw everybody off his scent. If they believed she had been kidnapped, then they would never suspect that she ran off with him. He had been snooping around the house all day waiting for the Ramseys to get home, so he probably saw some documentation from John's Christmas bonus and knew exactly how much money he could ask for. Plus, if he could find a way to actually collect the money, he and JonBenét could start their new life with $118,000. The note was so weird because the guy was weird. He had a very active fantasy life but was emotionally and intellectually immature.

After everybody in the Ramsey house went to bed, I think the killer sneaked into JonBenét's room and quietly woke her. Since she knew him and they had some sort of secret friendship, she did not panic. She went down to the kitchen with him and he told her the plan. She obviously didn't want to run away from her family, at which point the killer realized his plan was not going to work. He struck her in the head with something, rendering her unconscious, and carried her to the basement. There he acted out his violent fantasies and killed her. Then he covered her with a blanket, left her with her favorite nightgown, and snuck out of the house.

I don't know who the guy was and I'm not going to participate in the internet witch hunts to name him. That's the job of the police who are actually investigating the case. I don't think the killer was a master criminal, and I bet he left more than enough evidence to get caught. Had the crime scene been treated property, I bet that he would have been.

We were pretty hard on the Boulder Police Department and the Boulder District Attorney's office weren't we? Should we finish by saying something nice? You're right, we probably should.

The Boulder Police Department couldn't have done a worse job on the crime scene if they dispatched a diarrhetic goat to empty its bowels on the floor. The District Attorney's office was so accommodating of the prime suspects that it feels wrong they never even got a bribe out of the deal. (We're getting to the nice things, I promise.) They both did a really poor job initially. But the effort they put in after that was really impressive. They devoted more time and effort into this case than I've ever seen out of a department that size on a single homicide. And it was good work too. If the case could have been solved, I think they would have done it. Even aside from the problems they caused themselves with the crime scene debacle, they just couldn't catch a break. But they never quit trying.

Boulder is a small city of about 100,000 people, give or take. It's 25 miles from Denver, which is a big city with big city crime problems. But Boulder averages about 1 murder a year. A single murder per year for 100,000 people. The United States averages about 5 murders per 100,000 people per year. Denver averages about 9 per 100,000 people per year.

So far they've failed to solve the JonBenét homicide. They've solved most of the other ones, but even if they hadn't, can you blame them? They don't get much experience investigating homicides. People don't get murdered very often in Boulder and you have to give some credit to the Boulder criminal justice system for that. The ultimate job of the criminal justice system is to protect the community and you won't find a lot of communities safer than Boulder.

It takes good police work to solve murders but it takes better police work to prevent them. That's not the work we are doing here though. You and I are solving murders. We've gotten close enough on this one to call it a win, so let's move on to another.

Tupac and Biggie

We are off to a great start here. Two up and two down, just like that. People are going to start talking about us. But you know what worries me? Jealousy. You know how people are. They can't just be happy for our success. When they see the work we've done so far, you know they are going to be petty. "Of course you can work on murders of white girls," they'll say. "I've got the Lifetime Channel too," they'll say. To Hell with them. Let's put a stop to that right now. Let's solve the Tupac and Biggie murders. That will really shut them up.

But let's acknowledge our sources before we get into the details. Since there are actually two murders here, there is a little more homework than usual. The first text we are relying on is *LAbyrinth* by Randall Sullivan. Sullivan provides a great abbreviated history of Los Angeles gangs and hip hop music so that rural folks like myself can follow along. The second text is *Murder Rap: The Untold Story of the Biggie Smalls & Tupac Shakur Murder Investigations* by retired LAPD Detective Greg Kading. And lastly, we also will rely on *The Killing of Tupac Shakur* by former Las Vegas Sun reporter Cathy Scott.

I almost never recommend a movie over the book it was based on. I don't write movies and I imagine the people who do write them have enough money as it is. Spend that cash on books, I say, because old Barney Doyle has expensive tastes.

But if you can't get around to reading Greg Kading's book, I will offer an alternative. The USA Network series *Unsolved* presents essentially the same information and it is fantastic. Bear in mind, I am not a television critic and I am not qualified to pass judgment on the artistic merits of the show. I suspect it is actually pretty shitty in that regard. But it is fantastic nonetheless. Jimmi Simpson plays Detective Russell Poole like he's a long lost McPoyle brother off *It's Always Sunny in Philadelphia*. Wendell Pierce isn't given a single line worthy of the great Bunk Moreland, but still loans the show more credibility than it deserves. All of the famous characters look a little bit like they did in real life, but the dialogue and acting are so clunky that it feels like a cross between a Forensic Files reenactment and a Saturday Night Live sketch. One of the detectives looks more like Dave Chapelle than Dave Chapelle does. And Josh Duhamel's backwards hat is so distracting that I actually had to look up the costume designer to see what other work they've done. Eddie Gomez, if you were curious, and he worked on *Justified*, so he has performed better work with hats before.

If we had the time, we could have read 50 other books about these murders and watched a hundred documentaries on top of that. But who's got that kind of time? And we would have gotten 150 contradictory stories about what happened anyway. I am unaware of any other unsolved murder in the world that has been "solved" as many times as the Tupac and Biggie murders have. It seems the only people who have investigated these cases and not solved them are the police.

But enough about that, let's get to know the victims a little.

Tupac Shakur was one of the most successful musicians of the 1990s, in any genre. As it happens, his genre was gangsta rap. Since I am a middle-aged man, we will be referring to it as gangster rap from here on out.

His music was largely about inner city life during the latter stages of the 20th century. It was about gangs. It was about drugs. It was sometimes violent and often misogynistic. It rhymed in inventive and unexpected ways. It was embraced by a lot of young people and summarily dismissed by a lot of old people. It was extremely popular and continues to be so to this day. Whether you like the music or not, Tupac was a hugely successful and influential musician.

As a person, Tupac Shakur was extremely complicated. I suppose everybody is, but we don't get to know other strangers in quite the same way we get to know famous people. I took a college course on the literature of popular culture (one in a series of terrible investments by young Barney Doyle) and we read two books about Tupac Shakur. I was skeptical when I saw that section on the syllabus because I questioned what could be learned from the study of a life like Shakur's. I came away surprised. He lived a fascinating but troubled life and although most of his troubles were unique to that of a supremely talented artist in a brutal subsection of society, those troubles still resonated with me even if I couldn't directly relate.

Shakur was raised by a usually-single mother in New York, then Baltimore. His mother was an intellectual and a radical, but struggled with addiction and poverty. She still managed to get Tupac into a performing arts high school and he received what was by all accounts a top-notch education in the arts. I am not qualified to pass judgment on Tupac's intellect, but I feel comfortable saying that he had a far greater understanding of and appreciation for classical literature than I did. It should also be noted that I got a minor in English Literature from an accredited University, and he was a gangster rapper. So like I said, the man was complicated.

He moved to Los Angeles before his 18th birthday and became a success as a rapper and an actor before he was legally old enough to drink. But if his lyrics are to be believed, he may have tried an alcoholic beverage or two by that point. And possibly some marijuana.

Like a lot of young musicians, Tupac had disputes with his record label over his share of the revenue. And then he started getting into legal trouble. He racked up some assault charges. His name surfaced in the tragic accidental shooting of a six-year-old boy. He went to prison for sexual assault. He was shot five times as the victim in an apparent robbery, but survived. He signed with a record label founded by one convicted felon and reputedly financed by another. And eventually he died in the drive-by shooting that we are going to discuss shortly.

Erik Estrada played a California Highway Patrol Trooper for six years on the TV show CHiPS. He wasn't a cop, he was just an artist portraying one. But his portrayal made him famous and beloved and, lo and behold, he eventually became a sheriff's deputy in Virginia. He did not participate in the Tupac or Biggie murder investigations and this story is neither here nor there as far as our work is concerned, but I tell it as a preface for this: Tupac didn't grow up a gangster but he portrayed one as an artist. That portrayal made him famous and beloved. And eventually, he tragically died as one.

Christopher Wallace, The Notorious B.I.G., Biggie Smalls was also born to a single mother in New York City. One year after Tupac, as a matter of fact. Wallace was a high school dropout who sold drugs. But it would still be a stretch to call him a gangster. By most accounts he was a small-time drug dealer who aspired to be a rapper.

And boy did he succeed. He released his first album at 23 years old. It went platinum six times and earned him a Grammy nomination.

The Biggie nickname was not ironic, like when people call me "Slim" or "Handsome." Wallace was somewhere between three and four hundred pounds. But he was charming and, somehow, a bit of a sex symbol. Don't look at me like that. I'm not lying to you. I was a teenager in

1996, I had MTV, and I know that girls were into Biggie. He wasn't as conventionally attractive as Tupac, but women definitely saw something in him. God bless that era. Even old Barney Doyle scored a date for the senior prom.

But I digress. Tupac and Biggie were two of the most famous American musicians of that era. And their paths crossed frequently. Tupac lived in California and Biggie lived in New York, but they were friends early in their careers. They were competing acts on competing record labels, so the friendship hit some turbulence. Then it crashed and burned. Remember a little bit ago when I said Tupac survived a shooting in an apparent robbery? It was outside of a music studio on his way to meet Biggie. Tupac suspected that Biggie and his producer, Sean "Puffy" Combs, set him up. And it didn't help that Biggie released a song called "Who Shot Ya" not long after.

Tupac was signed to Death Row Records and Biggie to Bad Boy Records. There was a legitimate feud going on between Death Row and Bad Boy in the 1990s. They were both highly successful music labels, but it wasn't just a business feud. This wasn't Mr. Peanut and the Monopoly man tossing monocles at each other over Baltic Avenue. There were enough real gangsters associated with both labels that violence was a genuine concern. And in 1996, it came to fruition.

On September 7, 1996, Tupac was in Las Vegas for a Mike Tyson fight. After the fight, Tupac was to attend an event at Club 662, which was owned by Death Row

Records CEO Marion Knight. So as not to diminish my credibility on the streets, we will refer to Knight by his nickname, "Suge," from here on out.

Tupac, Suge and a large entourage were traveling to Club 662 a little after 11:00 p.m., going east on Flamingo Road. They stopped at a red light at Koval Lane, which is about a half-mile east of Caesar's Palace if you've ever been there. Because of the fight and because it was Las Vegas, there were a lot of vehicles on the road and a lot of pedestrians in the area.

Tupac was in the front passenger seat of a BMW driven by Suge. A bodyguard named Frank Alexander was riding in another car behind them with two rappers named Yafeu Fula and Malcolm Greenridge. Both vehicles were stopped in the second lane from the curb. A newer white Cadillac passenger car pulled up in the right-hand lane beside the BMW. A gun poked out the rear driver's side window and fired at least 13 rounds into the front passenger side door of the BMW. Tupac was hit in the chest, hip and hand. Suge was struck in the head by broken glass. The white Cadillac turned right on Koval Lane and sped away. Suge made a u-turn and drove like a wild man for about a mile before crashing the car into the median on the Las Vegas Strip.

Witnesses described four black men in the Cadillac. Alexander said that the shooter was wearing a skull cap. Despite thousands of potential witnesses, nobody managed to identify the shooter.

Tupac and Suge were both taken to the hospital for treatment. Suge was stitched up and released. Tupac died from his injuries six days later.

On March 8, 1997, Biggie was in Los Angeles for the Soul Train Music Awards and attended an after-party hosted by Vibe magazine at the Petersen Automotive Museum. The crowd got too big for the venue and spilled out onto the street. Eventually the fire marshal had to shut it down and the LAPD was called to help disperse the crowd.

Biggie, Puffy and their entourage left the party at a little after midnight on March 9, in a caravan of Chevrolet Suburbans and Blazers. Puffy rode in the front passenger seat of the lead vehicle with a driver and three bodyguards. Biggie rode in the front passenger seat of the second vehicle with four other rappers. A bodyguard/off-duty police officer named Reggie Blaylock drove the third vehicle with a passenger named Paul Offard.

All three vehicles were going north on Fairfax, but the last two SUVs got caught at a red light on Wilshire Boulevard. I've never been to Los Angeles, but on the map it is essentially right outside the Petersen Automotive Museum.

A white SUV traveling south on Fairfax made an abrupt u-turn and tried to cut in between Blaylock's Blazer and the Suburban Biggie was riding in. Blaylock pulled closer to cut the SUV off, then heard six gunshots in front of him. He saw a dark colored newer-model Chevrolet Impala on the passenger side of the Suburban and the Impala's driver holding a pistol out of the driver's side window.

The Impala turned east on Wilshire. Blaylock tried to chase it but quickly lost the car.

The lead Suburban turned back around to check on the shooting. Biggie had been hit four times and was dying in the front seat. Puffy jumped into the Suburban and they drove Biggie to the hospital, where he was pronounced dead.

Witnesses in the second Suburban said that the driver was alone in the Impala. None of the witnesses could identify the man but described him as a light-complected black man with a receding hairline. They also said he was wearing a bow tie.

I know we are here to solve murders and that you probably aren't interested in old Barney Doyle's thoughts on race and crime in America, but I'm going to get on my soapbox for a minute because it is relevant to this case.

There is a very complicated history between the police and the African American communities in this country. Even today there is a great deal of distrust and animosity on both sides. And certain factions of each group are eager to blame the other. Both sides have their reasons—some very legitimate and some imagined—but regardless, the fractured relationship is one of the greatest failures of modern law enforcement. I can't even imagine how difficult it must be for black police officers to navigate day-to-day life in their jobs and in their communities.

I grew up and learned to be a police officer in an area that was 99 percent white. If you asked 25-year-old Barney

Doyle who commits most of the crimes in this country he would tell you that it's nothing but honkeys. Had I grown up in and worked in certain areas of Compton, California, I'd tell you it was entirely black people. If I was from specific parts of Miami, Florida, I'd blame it all on Cubans. If I worked the north slope of Alaska, I'd be pointing the finger at Inuits and polar bears. It turns out that criminals commit almost all of the crimes and that criminals come from all colors and creeds.

Now let's go down the White Nationalist rabbit hole and look at some select statistics. According to the United States Department of Justice, black people accounted for 27.2% of all arrests in 2017. According to United States Census Bureau data, black people made up about 13.4% of the population at that time. One of those numbers is bigger than the other. A growing segment of loud and unpleasant people in this country insist that the numbers mean something fundamental about black people. I'd like to point out another number that I think is a lot more meaningful. According to the same United States Census Bureau data, 21.2% of black people in the United States lived in poverty in 2017. That was more than double the rate for white folks.

About the only race that has a higher rate of poverty than blacks is Native Americans. We will work on a fascinating reservation murder later, but just file this information away for now. I firmly believe that the United States is the greatest nation in the world and that our values of freedom, justice and democracy will stand the test of time. But we aren't even 250 years old yet. Black people were forced over to this country as slaves. Native Americans were dehumanized and slaughtered in a series of vicious wars. It is probably going to take more time and more effort on the part of the United States to make those two groups feel like they are an equal part of what we all want this country to be.

Now I'll let you in on a dirty little secret about policing: It's a whole lot easier to catch poor people committing crimes than it is rich people. If you are using drugs in a large home in a gated community then the police are rarely going to catch you. If you're doing it on the street corner or the trailer park, they just might. Unless you are breaking traffic laws in front of a cop, you probably aren't getting stopped in a newer car. But a lot of old junkers are rolling equipment violations that get stopped by the police every other day. Old Barney Doyle knows how to get to the bottom of a shoplifting complaint. I'm going to have a tough time with a securities fraud case.

I'm no sociologist and I won't pretend to know why poverty rates are higher for blacks. The most logical cause that I've read is the rampant housing discrimination that took place for decades starting after World War II. Most middle class families built their net worths through home ownership, but discriminatory lending practices denied a lot of blacks the same opportunities. I'm sure it is more complicated than I am painting it here, but I'm a cop not an academic. Do your own research if you want to know more. I am just setting the scene because we are going to talk about Los Angeles and the Los Angeles Police

Department in the 1990s. And we won't understand much about this story without at least a cursory understanding of the racial dynamics that seemed to frame everything in the Tupac and Biggie murder investigations.

The Los Angeles Police Department entered into a consent decree with the United States Department of Justice in 2001. If you aren't familiar with consent decrees, in the law enforcement world they are a mechanism by which extremely broken police departments get fixed by the federal government because the government decides the department cannot be trusted to fix itself. It involves a tremendous amount of oversight, red tape, bureaucracy and shame. It's an extraordinary measure that is only used for the most egregious cases, where systematic failures led to widespread abuses of civil rights. It's completely demoralizing for the departments involved and the surest sign I know that there is a disconnect between a department and the citizens it serves.

The LAPD consent decree followed decades of accusations of racial bias in how officers policed and how they used force. It also followed a series of high-profile scandals, including a bank robbery committed by one narcotics detective and a series of drug thefts from the evidence room by another narcotics detective. The murders of Biggie and Tupac (Tupac's murder took place in Las Vegas, but all of the players involved were from Los Angeles) occurred just five years after police were acquitted of criminal charges in the beating of Rodney King. If you were alive to see coverage of the riots that followed the verdict, then you know that a relationship that broken was not fixed in five years.

While the LAPD may not have inspired a lot of trust in the community they served, the organization did generate an unbelievable amount of paranoia and cynicism from within its own ranks. Both Russell Poole and Greg Kading went through all of the trouble of writing a book (no easy task, believe you me) where each accused the LAPD of trumping up misconduct charges against them because they were getting too close to solving the Biggie Smalls murder. The two investigations were ten years apart and came to wildly different conclusions about who committed the murder, but both men were certain enough that the LAPD was deliberately sabotaging them that they committed it to the page for everybody to see. That's a lot of paranoia. That's the kind of ranting and raving we're used to seeing from bearded guys on street corners or from weirdos on internet message boards. But these weren't deranged conspiracy theorists, they were decorated detectives for one of the largest police departments in the world. They were men of enough esteem within that department that they were assigned to an incredibly high-profile murder investigation.

And for the record, Russell Poole didn't write *LAbyrinth*. Randall Sullivan wrote the book and did a tremendous job in his research. But his account of Poole's investigation was clearly coming straight out of Poole's mouth.

On the other hand, the Las Vegas Police Department has publicly said that they believe they know who shot

Tupac, but have not been able to gather enough evidence to prosecute. They lay a lot of that blame on uncooperative witnesses, including Suge. Maybe they are telling the truth and maybe they are bluffing to put pressure on the killer. Either way, they know a hell of a lot more about the murder than they are sharing with the public (ballistic information, witness statements, results of neighborhood canvasses, information from informants, etc.). Good. That's how it's supposed to work. If you release every detail you know then you have no way to authenticate a confession down the road. As much as people have derided them for failing to arrest Tupac's murderer, I appreciate that they haven't let the victim's fame cause them to disregard basic investigative principles. Maybe they will clear the case someday and maybe they won't. But playing it close to the vest is the right move and I respect them for it.

Of course it kind of screws us here. I mean, you and I aren't really in a position to play the long game. We have to solve this by the end of the chapter. And we are running out of pages. It would be helpful to have a peek at some more of the evidence in this case, but oh well. We've thrown out some guesses before and I'm not above doing it again.

Russell Poole, who investigated the Biggie murder in 1997, believed that Suge Knight participated in the murder of Tupac and that he may have been assisted by LAPD or Compton Police Department officers in his employ.

Yes, Suge was sitting right beside Tupac when Tupac was shot and yes Suge took some shrapnel himself. But

Poole claims witnesses who knew Suge believed he was bold enough and fearless enough to arrange a hit on Tupac while he was in the car with him, if for no other reason than to throw suspicion off him.

The theory has a couple of things going for it. First of all, Suge was a legit gangster. He had a long rap sheet and was accused of a hundred other serious crimes that he was never charged with. As of this writing he is sitting in prison for manslaughter, so murder isn't that great of a stretch.

According to Sullivan's book, Suge and Tupac's relationship had soured in the months leading up to the shooting. Tupac signed with Suge's label when Tupac was in prison for rape, and Suge treated him like a star from the moment he got out. But Sullivan reported that Tupac was frustrated with how Suge ran the finances and that he intended to leave Death Row records when his contract was up. Sources also told Sullivan that Suge may have owed Tupac a lot of money in royalties and that Suge wasn't in a position to pay. The theory is that Suge killed Tupac to keep him from leaving Death Row and to keep from having to pay out royalties.

I've read various conflicting statements as to whether Suge actually owed Tupac money. I haven't balanced the books myself, so I have no idea. We'll consider it a reasonable motive if for no other reason than we lack reliable information to refute it.

Since Suge was driving the car when Tupac got shot, he was in a perfect position to see the shooter. But he didn't help the police identify the murderer of his supposed friend. This would make sense if Suge hired the shooter and didn't want to get caught. But Suge himself was shot six times in a crowded nightclub in 2014 and didn't tell the cops anything that time either. A TMZ report on the incident said that Suge wasn't going to be no snitch. So take that with a grain of salt. Maybe he didn't identify Tupac's shooter because he hired him. Maybe he didn't identify Tupac's shooter because he didn't know who it was. Or maybe he didn't identify Tupac's shooter because he's an asshole. All plausible theories at this point.

While Poole was conducting the Biggie investigation, and tangentially looking into related Tupac information, he found himself in or around a series of cases that involved LAPD officers who were much more criminals than they were cops. And Poole found some interesting circumstantial evidence suggesting that these cops and others were being paid by Suge and Death Row, even though the LAPD had explicitly barred officers from working side jobs for that company. It gained traction among some theorists that cops would be experts at getting away with murder. Since somebody had gotten away with the Tupac murder, they surmised that Suge hired LAPD officers to kill Tupac. But the Tupac shooting happened on a crowded street in front of half of Las Vegas. I doubt cops are actually that skilled at getting away with murder, but I still don't believe they would be so brazen as to do it in the open like that.

Greg Kading had a different and simpler theory on the Tupac murder. Suge, Tupac and Death Row records were associated with a subset of the Bloods street gang. Despite Puffy's repeated denials, Bad Boy was suspected of hiring members of the Crips street gang for various security duties. Suge and Puffy had a pretty nasty feud going and Puffy was starting to fear for his life. So Kading thinks that Puffy put a bounty out on Suge and Tupac. Plus, a Crip was beaten by Tupac and the Death Row crew at a casino earlier in the night. Kading believed that both led to the Tupac killing. A little bit of a contract hit and a little bit of a revenge hit.

Orlando Anderson was the name of the man who took the beating in Las Vegas. The official story is that it was spearheaded by Tupac himself and payback for an incident that happened in Los Angeles several weeks earlier. Anderson and some Crips supposedly stole the chain off the neck of somebody in Death Row's crew. Tupac and his Death Row entourage saw Anderson standing in a hotel lobby as they left the Tyson fight and jumped him. The fight was broken up by security and Anderson declined to press charges.

Anderson had an uncle by the name of Duane Davis who went by a street name that is either spelled Keffe D or Keefe D, depending on which source you believe. I'm going with Keefe, because Keffe just looks funny to me, even for a street name.

Keefe was with Anderson in Vegas but not at the time of the beating. Both men initially denied any involvement in the murder and Anderson was killed in a gang-related shooting in Los Angeles before his story changed. A decade after the murder, Keefe changed his story. He claimed that Anderson shot Tupac as revenge for the beating.

According to Keefe, he caught up with Anderson and a couple of other Crips after the beating and decided to shoot Tupac in retaliation. They initially staked out Club 662, but gave up when Tupac and Suge hadn't showed up. They were driving back from the liquor store when they saw Tupac hanging out of Suge's sunroof talking to some female fans. Keefe was in the front passenger seat and Anderson was in the rear passenger-side seat. They flipped a u-turn and worked their way through traffic to the passenger side of Suge's BMW. The man in the rear driver-side seat was supposed to shoot Tupac, but lost his nerve. Anderson took the gun, reached across the seat, and unloaded into the BMW. They then hauled ass out of there and stashed the gun and the Cadillac.

Keefe said that he would have shot Tupac himself if he had been in a better seat to take the shot. A little bit as revenge for the beating of his nephew, but mostly for the $1 million bounty that Puffy had put up. Suge blamed Puffy's people in the shooting death of one of Suge's friends outside of a club in Atlanta. And Tupac still blamed Biggie and Puffy for the shooting in New York. Having a man like Suge blame you for two shootings is a good way to end up on the wrong end of a shooting yourself. So Puffy sought out Keefe and a couple of other Crips to take care of it for him.

This is one of the only murders on our list where we have what amounts to a confession. Good enough for most people, I suppose. Our imitators and detractors would surely be satisfied to call the case solved on Keefe's story alone. But that's not us. We want the truth and we'll pursue it even in the face of several extra pages of work. That's what distinguishes us from those slapdash operations all over the internet.

Keefe's confession came during a negotiation with investigators and prosecutors. He was facing a substantial prison sentence for drug charges at the time. We know better than to take any story like that at face value, so let's examine what's right and wrong about Keefe's claims.

The most obvious thing Keefe's story has going for it is its simplicity. The easiest explanation isn't always the correct one, but a lot of the time it is. We know Orlando Anderson was in Vegas at the time of the shooting. We know that Anderson was affiliated with a rival gang. We know Anderson was assaulted by Tupac a few hours before the shooting. We know Anderson died in an apparent gang-related shooting less than two years later. On the surface at least, the story seems to hold water.

Keefe also seemed to get the details right about the actual shooting. He got the car right. He got the location right. He got the time right. He got the general circumstances of the shooting right. He described co-conspirators who were known to be in the area. I can't find any record of the Las Vegas Police confirming that Keefe got the gun right, but I also didn't read anything that said he got it wrong.

What incentive would Keefe have to lie? And not just lie, but implicate himself in a murder with a lie? As backward as this sounds, implicating himself in a murder was his best bet for avoiding a life sentence. His drug charge was a federal charge and involved enough weight that, with his prior record, he was probably going away forever, our drug laws being what they are and all. In a proffer session you get to confess and negotiate a deal, but the confession can't be used against you unless you agree to the deal. Whatever they offered him couldn't be worse than life. And it would probably be way short of life if he offered them something they wanted. He knew they wanted the Tupac and Biggie murders. Whether he was involved or not, he had three weeks from the time of the first meeting until the time of the proffer meeting to come up with a story they wanted to hear. And not to cast aspersions about a member of the California Bar Association, but he had the chance to refine the story with an attorney who would recognize any glaring issues with it.

Stop me if you've heard this from me already, but what did Keefe's confession really give us that we can corroborate independently and that wasn't already known? By the time of the confession, everybody already knew the time and location of the shooting. Everybody knew the description of the shooter's car and the direction it fled after the shooting. Everybody knew how many people were in the car. Everybody knew about the Anderson assault earlier in the night. Sure, it all fit Keefe's story. But he could have gotten all of those details off the internet and adapted his story to fit them.

It's hard to corroborate most stories ten years after the fact, but Keefe's story was especially difficult to verify. All three of the other people he identified as being in the Cadillac at the time of the shooting, including Anderson, were dead. If he was spinning a line of bullshit, then of course he would pick a bunch of witnesses who couldn't contradict him.

I have three major points of contention with Keefe's story that don't make sense to me. The first: the shooting happened in Las Vegas not Mayberry. The street was packed with cars and people. Keefe and his crew just happened to find Tupac out driving, managed to flip a u-turn on a crowded street, then worked their way through traffic to get beside Suge's car? That's one hell of a lucky break for Keefe.

In an interview for a documentary, Keefe claimed that they saw Tupac hanging out of the sunroof of Suge's car talking to another car full of women. I haven't heard any other witness say that Tupac was ever hanging out of the sunroof. That seems like the kind of relevant detail that the bodyguard behind him would have noted. Other than 1980s movies, how many times have you actually seen somebody standing up through the sunroof of a car?

My second big issue with Keefe's story is the origin of the Cadillac. He said that it was rented by Anderson. Rental cars leave the kinds of paper trails that are super easy to follow. Anderson was a suspect right away in the investigation and I am confident that the Las Vegas Police knew exactly what he drove to Vegas. If it was a white

Cadillac, the LVPD would have found that vehicle right away and the forensic team would have gone over every inch of it. The fact that Anderson was never arrested tells me that he never rented a white Cadillac that weekend.

I also don't understand why Keefe participated in a super high profile murder-for-hire and never really concerned himself with collecting the million dollar bounty. He went to prison not long after Tupac's murder, but why didn't he try to collect before? Or after he was released? It's a million dollars. I just don't see the type of person willing to murder a celebrity as being the same type who would let a million dollar debt go for no good reason.

For what it's worth, Puffy obviously denies that he ever put a bounty on Suge and Tupac. But we'd expect him to deny it whether he did or not. There is no evidence against him and most people don't publicly confess to felonies that couldn't otherwise be proven.

For the sake of calling it solved, let's throw out a guess that fits as many of the facts as we can. There was no attempt to take anything, so this wasn't a robbery. The shooting was isolated to a single vehicle, so it wasn't a random mayhem type shooting. The victim was extremely famous and the shooter undoubtedly would have recognized him, so it seems likely that he was the specific target. There were four people in the suspect vehicle, so logic suggests that it was a gang shooting.

Not to besmirch the dead, but Anderson is our best bet for the gunman. He was associated with a rival gang. He had been involved in a prior assault/robbery with Death

Row members. And he had been assaulted by Tupac the night of the murder. He hits all the high points we are looking for in a gang shooting.

I don't buy the Puffy bounty theory for the reasons we already discussed, but I am willing to entertain the idea that money was a motive in the shooting. Poole was convinced that Suge put out the hit on Tupac. It's crazy on the surface to think that he would arrange to have somebody essentially shoot at him. But if you can get past that major flaw in the logic, the rest is interesting. Anderson didn't press charges in the beating. Security described him as extremely calm about the incident and a bodyguard with Tupac's crew said it almost looked like Anderson was willing and waiting to take the beating. Anderson also later testified on Suge's behalf at a parole hearing, suggesting that Suge didn't participate in the beating even though surveillance video pretty much showed that Suge did. It sure sounds like money exchanged hands between the two for something.

Keefe claimed that he was in the front passenger seat of the Cadillac and looked Suge in the face right before the shooting. The two men knew each other well and Suge could have identified Keefe if he wanted to. But he didn't. Yeah, yeah, I know: Suge ain't no snitch. But I'll let you in on another little police secret. Everybody is a snitch. Especially people who claim they aren't. Gangsters only have integrity in TV shows. In real life, they are cold-hearted capitalists. They do what's in their best interest. If snitching can get them out of prison a few days earlier, they'll snitch. Unless snitching will get them killed. Then they do a cost-benefit analysis to weigh the danger versus the years. Risk management at its finest. Real gangsters are more Wall Street than anybody on Wall Street.

Suge did nine years on the parole violation and he probably wouldn't have done any of that time if he had snitched on Tupac's killer. Since he didn't, we can assume that he either legitimately didn't know the shooter or determined that the cost of snitching was too high. Since we already guessed that Anderson was the shooter, and Suge knew Anderson, we are moving on to scenario two. The cost was too high. Nothing I read about Suge suggests that he feared retaliation. But if he paid Keefe and Anderson to kill Tupac, then obviously he couldn't snitch on them. They'd all go to prison for life.

And if Suge paid Tupac's killer, then that explains how they were able to find Suge's car on a crowded Las Vegas street on a Saturday night. He would have tipped them off and made it easy for them.

It's a fun theory (for everybody but Suge I guess), but it does require you to suspend some disbelief. Is anybody really crazy enough to hire a hitman to shoot the guy sitting six inches from them? I'm going to believe it just because the story is way more fun and interesting if Suge is some sort of fearless gangster mastermind. But if you aren't willing to go that far, I understand. The theory makes just as much sense if Anderson shot Tupac for all of the other reasons we described. It's probably a cleaner theory that way, I'll give you that much. It's just not as fun.

Now onto Biggie.

Detective Poole went to, unfortunately, his grave believing that Los Angeles Police Department detectives participated in the Biggie murder. He told everybody who would listen. When people stopped listening, he believed the department was covering it up. Eventually he didn't trust his supervisors, his supervisors didn't trust him, and the situation spiraled until Poole resigned. He died of a heart attack several years later while trying, in vain, to get the Los Angeles Sheriff's Office to investigate his claims.

At the heart of the Poole theory are three former LAPD Detectives named Kevin Gaines, David Mack and Rafael Pérez. Gaines was actually killed nine days after Biggie in the type of convoluted tragic misunderstanding that can only happen in a department as messed up as the LAPD was. Gaines was off duty when he got into a road rage altercation with another plainclothes LAPD detective named Frank Lyga. It escalated until Lyga shot Gaines dead. Lyga was white and Gaines was black and the shooting touched every raw nerve the city had leftover from the Rodney King disaster.

Poole led the Lyga/Gaines investigation and discovered a web of ties between LAPD detectives and Death Row Records. For starters, Gaines was a married man, but when he was shot, he was driving a car that belonged to a woman who was not his wife. The woman was Suge Knight's wife, Sharitha Knight. Sharitha was also Gaines' girlfriend. She and Suge were estranged so I won't judge her too much for the arrangement. Gaines was supposedly happily married with children, so feel free to judge him as harshly as you like.

David Mack worked in the LAPD Rampart Division's notorious and controversial Community Resources Against Street Hoodlums (CRASH) unit that, depending on whose account you believe, was an innovative and effective street crime deterrent and/or one of the most ruthless gangs of criminals on the streets of Los Angeles.

Mack was an Olympic-caliber sprinter before joining the LAPD and a world-class bank robber afterward. He orchestrated a robbery that took over $700,000 from a Bank of America branch in Los Angeles in 1997. For perspective, most bank robberies rarely get more than a few thousand dollars. But most are committed by desperate drug addicts and not college-educated law enforcement officers who happen to be dating a bank employee.

Mack was eventually caught. He did 13 years in prison and much of the stolen money was never recovered. He had to have had at least two co-conspirators, including a getaway driver, but only his girlfriend who worked in the bank was ever positively identified. Poole suspected that Mack was aided by Rafael Pérez, another CRASH detective.

Pérez and Mack knew each other and Pérez was definitely more of a criminal than he was a cop, so it isn't a stretch to think that he helped Mack on the bank robbery. Pérez eventually went to prison for selling cocaine that he had stolen from various LAPD evidence rooms. He tried to cut a deal with prosecutors by providing the names of dirty cops. He made accusations about almost every cop in the Rampart CRASH unit for everything from brutality to planting evidence to murder. He was probably lying about most of it to save his own skin, but some of it was probably true too. That's the problem with liars. We just can't read too much into anything they say.

Pérez never said a thing about either the Biggie or the Tupac murders, but Poole believed Pérez and Mack were involved in at least the planning of the Biggie murder. He found some circumstantial evidence to suggest that Gaines, Mack and Pérez all secretly worked for Death Row and, by proxy, the Bloods street gang.

Mack had a close friend from his track days by the name of Amir Muhammad who bore a striking resemblance to a composite sketch of Biggie's shooter. A prison snitch had also told investigators that Biggie was shot by a man with the name Amir or Ashmir. Mack also had a Chevy Impala and Poole found evidence suggesting that Mack was at the Petersen Automotive Museum on the night of the murder. Poole believed that the LAPD commanders were obstructing him from pursuing the leads further.

Kading's theory was that the Biggie murder was ordered by Suge in retaliation for the Tupac murder. Kading believed that a Blood member by the name of Wardell "Poochie" Fouse committed the murder on Suge's behalf. Informants had described Poochie as an enforcer for Suge and Death Row. He had an Impala, but so did half of the young black men in Los Angeles at the time, from the sounds of things. His name came up in jailhouse chatter as Biggie's shooter and he eventually died in a shooting in 2003 that was believed to be gang related.

Kading was working on leveraging a criminal charge against one of Suge's female acquaintances into some information. Theresa Swann was very reluctant, so Kading concocted a ruse where he forged a confession letter and claimed that Poochie wrote it before he died. Swann read the letter and said that Poochie was telling the truth. Kading believed the matter was solved. His bosses and the prosecutors disagreed.

We wouldn't trust a confession under those circumstances, so we certainly aren't going to humor a statement that was completely fabricated by police just because it was agreed to by a criminal with every incentive to lie. Maybe Poochie did shoot Biggie, but what Kading did isn't evidence.

Kading's book also briefly mentions another theory in which Keefe D and the Crips shot Biggie. To his credit, Kading dismissed that theory pretty quickly. Man, Keefe's name pops up in everything. If it hadn't happened three years before his birth, I'm sure somebody would put him on the grassy knoll for the Kennedy shooting too.

Keefe D was at the Peterson Auto Museum the night of the shooting, but that's as close to a connection as I can find to the shooting. There was some loose street talk about a conflict between Puffy and the Crips over security work, but it's too weak to consider here, even in a story as convoluted as this one. Maybe we can tie Keefe to another murder later in the book if we run out of options, but I say we let him off the hook for Biggie.

OK, I'll admit, my head hurts on this one. Usually we struggle with a murder investigation because we don't have enough information. Here we have way too much. And most of it is garbage. Street talk? Known associates? Third-hand eyewitness accounts? This is not how we solve murders. Let's disregard as much as we can and work our way through the rest to come up with a theory that works.

The Biggie murder was a true hit. The shooter worked alone. He picked a car that could blend into the environment. He did the deed quickly and got the hell out of there. He wore a classy bowtie. He was a professional. Professionals work for money, so somebody paid to have Biggie killed.

On first reading, I was certain that the white SUV who cut through traffic and distracted the bodyguard had to have been involved in the murder. The timing was too perfect to be a coincidence. The car flipped a u-turn to catch up to the convoy and then tried to slide right between Biggie's Suburban and his bodyguard's Blazer, blocking security's view of the shooting in the process. Then it took off after the shooting and a witness several blocks away saw a vehicle matching that description going the same direction as the suspect vehicle. That is a lot of coincidences.

But Kading managed to track down the driver and the passenger for interviews. They each insisted that they were hanging around the Biggie entourage trying to pitch some sort of business venture and that they had nothing to do with the murder. The Three Stooges timing was just tragic luck. I don't know if I believe them. I wouldn't believe them at all except for two things: 1) Kading believed them, and he was the one who did the interviews and he is not an idiot. 2) neither man had any meaningful gang ties or criminal history before or after the murder.

With those two involved, it's a highly-choreographed criminal conspiracy. Without their involvement, it's just a successful murder-for-hire. The first scenario requires the kind of tactical planning and timing that might exceed the capabilities of a run-of-the-mill gangbanger. The kind of expertise a narcotics detective might have. But the second scenario? That could be any marginally skilled hitter. Biggie was over 300 pounds with an affinity for flashy colorful suits. It was a public street. He wasn't a particularly hard target.

From his dress, the shooter wanted witnesses to believe he was affiliated with the Nation of Islam. Maybe he was. There is a certain archetype of the black Muslim hitman, most famously portrayed by Brother Mouzone in *The Wire*. And the Nation of Islam had a certain reputation for organized and militant violence, especially back in that era. But I don't know how founded that reputation actually is in reality.

It seems more likely to me that the outfit was just the shooter's way of screwing with police. He knew he was going to be seen. He wanted to give witnesses something to describe other than his face. The only thing that draws the eye more than a pistol is a handsome bow tie. Plus, it had the added benefit or forcing police to go question a bunch of Nation of Islam members who already hated the LAPD.

I don't know if the shooter was Poochie, David Mack's track buddy or one of hundreds of hired guns in Los Angeles whose names I will never know. Who really cares? Do you give credit to the hammer that drove the nail, or the carpenter who was swinging it? Really? Neither of them? Let's not get snobbish just because we are solving famous murders here. Blue collar workers are people too.

It was probably Suge that ordered the hit on Biggie. I know I already blamed him for Tupac. I acknowledge that I look lazy right now. But I just can't see a more plausible scenario. He was a legit gangster. He had a real feud with Biggie and Puffy. And true or not, there were a lot of people out there blaming Bad Boy for the Tupac murder. Even if Suge was secretly behind the Tupac murder, there was no way he could allow the story on the street to be that he failed to avenge Tupac's death.

Or Keefe did it. From this point forward, let's consider Keefe a suspect for everything until we can prove otherwise.

Kimberly Nees

We stepped outside of our comfort zone with that last one. It involved a lot of famous figures, a lot of wealthy people and too many conspiracies to keep straight. It was fun and I feel like we grew because of the experience, but that's not our wheelhouse. That was a side project to show our critics the depth of our skills. It's time to get back in the pocket. This next one is where we excel: a tragic and brutal murder of a promising young woman, a bungled crime scene investigation, a controversial confession, a convicted murderer proclaiming his innocence, two future governors as prosecutors, an off-brand version of The Innocence Project and two *Dateline* specials. This is why we got into this business.

Our geographic setting is Poplar, Montana. Contrary to what you are picturing right now, Poplar is not the middle of nowhere. It is an hour away from the middle of nowhere. In 2016, the Washington Post used data from Oxford University to find the town in the contiguous United States that was farthest away from any metropolitan area. Glasgow, Montana was the winner and dubbed by the Washington Post as the official "Middle of Nowhere." The neighboring towns of Scobey and Wolf Point finished in second and third place. Poplar sits right among those places on the map, but only has a population of about 800 and thus didn't meet the Washington Post's criteria for a "town."

Our historical setting is 1979. I hadn't yet arrived in the world in 1979, so I will defer to those who were there on what the period was actually like. If movies and television are to be believed, 1979 was populated mostly with teenagers and young adults who were coming of age in an era of canned beer, faded denim and abundant marijuana against a background of bluesy rock music and general dread about the 1980s. Maybe you know better, so picture it however you deem appropriate. Don't try to tell me you were there though. Hogwash. With those looks? You aren't a day past 25.

But anyway, the tragic hero of our story was a young lady by the name of Kimberly Nees. She was just 17 years old in 1979. Every newspaper article about her death points out that she was beautiful and the published photographs certainly support the notion. She was the valedictorian of Poplar High School in 1979 and reputedly very popular in the way you would expect a nice, pretty and smart girl to be in a small town.

Poplar is on the southern border of the Fort Peck Indian Reservation and headquarters for the Fort Peck Assiniboine and Sioux Tribes. I have spent a fair amount of time on Native American reservations in Montana, including that one. You will occasionally hear reservations depicted as third-world hellholes where poverty, addiction and violence swallow up everything and everybody. They aren't that. Not by a long shot. The Fort Peck Indian Reservation is poor, like a lot of Reservations, but so is most of Montana. There are serious problems with addiction on the Fort Peck Reservation, but there are serious problems with addiction in most of rural America. The violent crime rate isn't much different on the Fort Peck Reservation than it is in any other place in America with a similar economic profile.

The refrain I have heard too much in my life from too many otherwise reasonable people is that "it is depressing to go to the reservation." Poplar is a small town. There are poor people, there are wealthy people and there are people who fall all over the spectrum in between. Folks work their jobs, raise their families and live their lives. Too many are addicted to alcohol. Opiates and methamphetamine are a serious problem. A frustrating number of businesses are empty and properties rundown. But those are the problems of any small town. Maybe they are bigger problems on the reservation, but I doubt the casual observer would even notice a difference if towns like Poplar didn't carry the stigma of being on a reservation.

I won't pretend to be an expert on the culture of any Native American tribe, but I lived in Montana long enough to understand that tension exists between Natives and whites. How could it not, given the history of how they came to coexist? It's not so much tension that it prevents friendships or causes outward hostility, but it can cause distrust and suspicion. Go to a state basketball tournament and it's almost palpable during a close game between a Native and non-Native team. The poor refs are getting dog-cussed as racists from both sides the entire night, no matter how evenly they call it. And that's a basketball game, not a murder.

I have a hard time relating as a homely middle-aged man, but I'm sure being a pretty teenage girl comes with its own set of challenges. As would growing up on the reservation with light skin. As would growing up in rural Montana in the 1970s. By all accounts, Kimberly Nees seemed to be navigating those challenges beautifully and on her way to great success in life. Until the tragic events of June 15, 1979. (Pause and imagine the Dateline commercial break music right now to set the mood.)

Nobody has written the definitive book on the Kimberly Nees murder (if you are looking for a book idea of your own), so we will be basing this on other sources. Most of the information comes directly from court filings related to a series of appeals by the man who was ultimately convicted of the murder. There are also a smattering of police reports posted online on a website called "Montanans For Justice," a series of newspaper articles in the *Billings Gazette* and some propaganda, er, research from Centurion Ministries.

The general facts of the case are as follows:

On the evening of June 15, 1979, Kimberly Nees went on a date to the drive-in movie theater in Poplar with her boyfriend, Greg Norgaard. They went in

Norgaard's car, and he took her home afterward sometime around midnight or 12:30 a.m. Greg was 21 years old and Kimberly was 17. They had been "going steady" for about six months, but were not on the best of terms that day. We'll talk more about that later. The short version is that Greg dropped Kimberly off at home and then went to the American Legion bar. Kim got in her truck and went driving.

I'm sure it's different now since teenagers carry devices in their pockets that contain video games, rock music and billions of pictures of naked people, but back in the olden days of Barney Doyle's youth, teenagers in small towns wore out the asphalt driving back and forth from one end of Main Street to the other. We called it "dragging Main." I think my parents called it "cruising Main." It probably dates back generations before that. But this isn't an anthropology book on the social habits of ancient American teenagers. This is a murder book. Let's get back to the murder.

Kim was out cruising Poplar that night and was seen by multiple other teenagers who were doing the same thing. According to at least two witnesses, Kim was parked at the gas station sometime before 1:00 a.m. She was alone in her father's pickup truck. One of those witnesses saw that same pickup traveling west on Highway 2 at about 1:00 a.m., but couldn't tell how many people were in the truck at that time.

At about 4:15 a.m., Tribal Police Officers Alfred Lizotte and Calvin Red Thunder observed a truck parked by a train bridge at the Poplar River west of town just off of Highway 2. It was a popular spot for teenagers to park and engage in 1970s teenage shenanigans, so the officers did not think much of it. When the truck was still there at 7:00 that morning, the officers drove down to investigate.

The officers discovered blood and hair inside the truck. Next to both the driver's side and the passenger's side of the pickup there were what Lizotte described in his testimony as "scuffle marks" where the dirt was kicked up. Approximately ten feet from the passenger side of the truck was what appeared to be a blood spot. Red Thunder observed drag marks leading away from the scuffle marks, and the officers followed these marks to the edge of the bank of the river. From there, the officers saw Nees' body, floating face-up in two feet of water about ten feet from the lower river bank.

Two patrol officers are not enough to handle a crime scene like that, so Lizotte and Red Thunder called for assistance. But Poplar is a bit of a jurisdictional anomaly. As mentioned earlier, Lizotte and Red Thunder worked for the Tribal Police Department. But Poplar is in Roosevelt County so the Roosevelt County Sheriff's office can also investigate crimes that occur there. The Fort Peck Reservation is federal land and the Bureau of Indian Affairs investigates most crimes on reservations. But the Federal Bureau of Investigation usually assists on anything as serious as a murder. Every one of those agencies got called in for the Nees murder but nobody seemed to know exactly who was in charge. Consequently, the scene got trampled, evidence was contaminated and the various entities involved have spent decades blaming each other for the debacle.

Forensic Pathologist Dr. John Pfaff conducted the autopsy and determined that Kimberly had suffered a brutal beating death. There were numerous lacerations to her head that went through her scalp all the way to her skull. There were also skull fractures that left bone fragments embedded in Kimberly's brain tissue. There were also defensive wounds to Kimberly's hands and arms and an abrasion on her back. Kimberly was dead before she was placed in the water and there was no evidence of sexual intercourse.

I am going to try to describe the crime scene and evidence in as orderly and lucid a fashion as I can. But I have to warn you, this is a convoluted crime scene, even by our standards. I mentioned earlier that this scene was bungled right? If you don't believe me, let's hear from the first of our two future Montana governors who appear in the story.

Then Deputy Attorney General Mark Racicot said in his closing arguments at the trial for the man convicted of the murder, "It was quite unusual for a prosecutor to stand up and say that the investigation was all screwed up. Well it may be unusual, but that is the truth. It was all screwed up."

So let's get screwy.

At the crime scene, Officers found that Kimberly's driver's side door was open but the passenger door was locked. There were no keys in the truck, the gear shift was in park, the radio was on, there were three gouge marks in the ceiling with hair hanging out of them and gouge marks on the steering wheel.

Officers found a three-foot, crescent-shaped, semi-circle of blood approximately nine feet from the right rear truck tire, but there was no blood trail from the passenger side of the vehicle. There were small spots of blood all around the exterior of the pickup.

There was a sweater and a purse on the ground beside the passenger door. Some sources claim that the sweater was neatly folded, which is a damn peculiar thing in a bloody crime scene. But it didn't look neatly folded in the one crime scene photo I've seen published online. It's not a great photo, but it kind of just looks like it fell on the ground to me. But "not a great photo" is going to be a recurring theme in this one.

There was also a partial palm print in blood on the passenger's side door. If you've heard anything about this case before you've probably heard about the palm print. It has never been matched to the man who was convicted of the murder. It has never been matched to any of the group of girls who were long rumored to have killed Kimberly. It has never been matched to anybody. And it probably won't be.

I am admittedly and shamefully not a fingerprint expert. I should be. It's such a useful discipline. But it's delicate work and I am a bit of a bull in a China shop. Everything I know about fingerprints tells me that the palm print left at the scene is not and won't ever be suitable for proper comparison. The fingerprints that you and I leave on our phones and beer cans are an oil that is transferred from our skin. Fingerprint powder sticks to that oil, and then the pattern can be lifted with tape. Sometimes you don't even need powder to see the pattern and the oil alone can be lifted with tape. A fingerprint that is collected in that manner can be preserved indefinitely for comparison. But blood doesn't behave like oil. You can't dust it and lift it without obliterating the print. So you have to take photographs of the fingerprint to use for comparison. The trick, to work best, is the photograph has to meet very specific criteria. It has to be taken at an exact right angle and at the proper size ratio.

The photographs I've seen do not look to me like they would work for comparison. Maybe enterprising analysts might find a way to make the photograph work, but I'm not holding my breath. I think the bloody palm print is a lost cause.

From the truck to the riverbank was about 250 feet, according to a sketch prepared by investigators. It was a steep 10' drop to the river from there. In addition to the drag marks, investigators also found spots of blood and hair along the trail.

Investigators found and photographed numerous shoe impressions, but did so after law enforcement was already trampling random shoe impressions about the crime scene. Almost none of the impressions was ever definitively linked to anybody, but we can assume that most of them belonged to law enforcement. Officers also observed lots of beer cans, trash and other debris. They collected some of it, seemingly at random, and it was haphazardly secured at the various departments with no apparent rhyme or reason.

Dr. Pfaff determined that the injuries were caused by a weapon, but he could not initially determine what that weapon was. With all of the blood, hair and gouge marks inside the truck, investigators determined that at least part of the assault took place in the cab of the truck. If you've ever been in a single-cab 1970s GMC pickup, you know there is not a lot of room. So the weapon had to have been hard enough to fracture a skull but small enough to swing in the cab of a truck.

A dive team searched the river and discovered a discarded hammer, which sure sounds like one of the few things that matches both of the criteria we identified above for the murder weapon. It's hard and it doesn't require much room. But Dr. Pfaff examined the hammer, compared it to the injuries and determined that the hammer was not used to kill Kimberly. It was just a random hammer tossed in the river at some unknown time and discovered near the scene of a vicious beating death. One of those coincidences that you and I hate so much.

When the vehicle was returned to Kimberly's father, he was asked to check for anything that might be missing. Kimberly's father looked through a toolbox in the back of the truck and determined that a 12-inch metal crescent wrench was missing. Dr. Pfaff compared that type of wrench to the injuries and determined that the wrench could have caused some, but not all, of Kimberly's injuries. If the wrench was involved, then a second weapon would have to have been used as well.

In a typical murder investigation, one agency takes custody of all the evidence from the crime scene. You have to establish a chain showing whose custody the evidence was in from the time it left the scene until the moment it showed up in court, and that's just easier when it all goes to the same evidence room. That didn't happen in this case. It seems like everybody took a little bit of evidence and stored it in places that aren't conventionally thought of as an evidence room. Case in point, some of the evidence was kept in the city judge's chambers at Poplar City Hall. Naturally, somebody broke into the judge's chambers at some point while the evidence was being stored there. It was a Poplar Police Department Officer by the name of Steve Grayhawk who, according to court testimony, kicked in the door, breaking the hasp, because he had to use the restroom. Again, if I may quote former Montana Governor Mark Racicot, "it was all screwed up."

Investigators quickly turned their attention to Norgaard, Kimberly's boyfriend, which is an obvious place to start in any murder investigation. And investigators learned right away about some troubles between Norgaard and Kim. Norgaard and Kim lived a couple of houses away from each other. Late on the afternoon of June 15, Norgaard saw Kim arriving home and asked her to come speak with him. According to Norgaard, Kim looked tired.

When Norgaard asked why, Kim said that she had been out driving until 4:30 a.m. the previous night with another boy named Steve Schagunn. Norgaard admitted that he was hurt when Kim told him about it. But Norgaard and Kim went on their date anyway.

Before the date, Norgaard went to the store to buy some beer and saw Steve's girlfriend. Norgaard told her about what Kim and Steve had done the night before and that he was "pissed a little."

Norgaard told investigators that he and Kim went on their date without really discussing Steve, but that Norgaard was still upset about the situation. So he took Kimberly home at around midnight and told her that he was going to the Legion Club bar. He did not walk her to the door and never saw her again.

Norgaard and multiple witnesses all said that he was at the Legion Club bar that night. He told investigators he left at about 1:30 a.m. and drove around town a few times looking to see if Kim was out driving. He drove by her house at about 2:00 a.m. and saw her truck was gone. He used a payphone at the Poplar Motel to call Kim's house. Kim's mother answered and Norgaard asked if she was home. Kim's mother said that she was not and asked Norgaard to look for her. He drove around until approximately 2:45 a.m. or 3:00 a.m., then gave up and went home. Norgaard said he never went by the train bridge.

Norgaard called another girl named Kathryn Moe at about 1:45 a.m. from the same payphone. According to Norgaard, he called Kathryn after speaking to Kim's mother. He called because they used to date and he wanted Kathryn to come out that night, partly to make Kim jealous. According to Kathryn, Norgaard spoke very casually and never really said why he called. Kathryn did not think Norgaard sounded drunk and he didn't mention anything about Kim Nees.

Norgaard also told investigators that several weeks before Kim's death, while Norgaard was away at college, he received an anonymous letter claiming that Kim had been out riding around with an ex-boyfriend. Norgaard said he asked Kim about it and she admitted that she had been.

Schagunn and his girlfriend, Suzie Kirn, were out together the night of June 15, and Schagunn remembered seeing Norgaard and Kim together early in the evening. Schagunn later saw Kimberly alone in her truck parked at the gas station at around 12:30 or 1:00 a.m. He saw Norgaard's car parked at the Legion Club at about 1:30 a.m.

Deputy Errol "Red" Wilson was one of several officers who canvassed homes in the vicinity of the train bridge looking for potential witnesses. He spoke to a woman named Roberta Clincher on June 16. Roberta told Deputy Wilson that she did not hear anything unusual that morning but that her teenage son, Barry Beach, had returned home early that morning covered in blood. Beach told Clincher that the blood came from punching his car in frustration after it got stuck in the sand at the swimming hole.

Clincher later denied that she said any such thing and Deputy Wilson did not write any reports that referenced the statement. But Deputy Wilson claimed that he notified the sheriff immediately after he spoke to Clincher and that he would not forget a conversation like that, regardless of whether he wrote a report.

Once again, I will refer you to former Governor Racicot. "Screwed up."

Beach was a troubled young man who dated Kimberly's younger sister, Pam. He was 17 years old at the time of Kim's death and lived a few hundred yards from the train bridge. He moved to Louisiana to live with his father and stepmother not too long after Kim's death.

Beach was just one of many suspects. The FBI was pursuing a theory that Norgaard may have killed Kimberly. They conducted at least two interviews with him. He denied any involvement in her death and investigators never found any direct evidence linking him to the crime.

The rumor around town was that a group of teenage girls killed Kimberly Nees because they were jealous of her. The girls are referred to as a "pack of girls" in much of the press coverage surrounding this case. We're discussing a bunch of young Native American women and the term "pack" carries too many racist overtones for my comfort. And I'm not usually perceptive to subtle racism, so it must not be all that subtle. We'll call them a group of girls for our purposes and we'll get to know them later in the story.

The investigation went nowhere productive for three-and-a-half years. Then police in Louisiana got an out-of-nowhere confession from Beach in January of 1983 and he was sentenced to 100 years without parole in the spring of 1984. Don't worry, that's barely the midpoint of our story, not the conclusion.

Beach went to the Ouachita Parish Sheriff's Office jail in Louisiana on January 4, 1983 for a minor offense. He was "contributing to the delinquency" of a child by helping his stepsister and her friends skip school. He escalated it to a bigger offense the following day when he called his stepmother from jail and threatened to kill her for turning him in. So she told the Louisiana police that Beach was a suspect in a murder in Montana. As fate would have it, the local authorities were investigating three other murders of their own, also young women, and Beach was as good as any suspect they had at the time.

The Ouachita Parish Sheriff's Office contacted the Roosevelt County Sheriff's Office in Pace Montana and confirmed that Beach was in fact a bona fide suspect in an unsolved murder. With Roosevelt County's blessing, Ouachita Parish Sheriff's Office Sergeant Jay Via and Commander Alfred Calhoun questioned Beach at the Sheriff's Office for somewhere between 6 and 10 hours. Beach initially denied killing Nees, but eventually gave a detailed confession of the crime. He repeated it several more times over the following weeks, including in the presence of his attorney.

Beach's confession goes generally as follows:

Beach was partying with two friends at a place called Sandy Beach on the afternoon of June 15, 1979. Beach got his car stuck in the sand, then ruined his transmission trying to get it out. He was angry and his friends tried to calm him down, but it didn't work. At about 4:30 p.m. he left his friends and walked back into town.

When he got home, he took a nap and didn't wake until sometime after dark. He then walked into town and saw Kim sitting alone in her truck at the Exxon gas station. Beach asked Kim if she knew where her sister Pam was, then asked if he could ride around with her. She let him, so they drove aimlessly around Poplar for a while before parking at the train Bridge.

Kim and Beach sat in her truck smoking weed and talking for a while and then Beach asked Kim to have sex with him. She refused, so he had her smoke some more weed in hopes that she would change her mind. Beach then tried to kiss her and she told him to get out of the truck. He refused and asked why girls didn't like him. Kim informed Beach that girls didn't like him because he was an "asshole." Beach then tried to grab Kim and she slapped him. They carried on like this for a little bit before Beach punched Kim, then picked up a crescent wrench from the floorboard and started hitting Kim in the head.

Kim tried to escape out the driver's side, but Beach got out the passenger side, ran around and pinned her against the truck before she could get away. He tried to kiss her again and she scratched him. So Beach started choking her. He had dropped the crescent wrench when he got out of the truck, so he grabbed a tire iron from the bed of the truck and started beating her in the head. Kim tried to run away, but Beach tackled her on the other side of the pickup and continued to beat her in the head. She tried to cover her head with her hands, but eventually stopped moving.

Beach checked her pulse and found that it was weak, and then it stopped. He realized that he'd killed her and started to panic. He decided that he needed to get rid of the evidence and tossed the wrench and the tire iron into the river. He then found a large garbage bag in the truck and tried to put Kim in it. She only partially fit in the bag, but he dragged her over to the river and pushed her in. He then took the keys from the truck and tossed them in the river. For some reason he picked Kim's jacket off the ground and threw it in the river beside her for good measure. Then he used his shirt sleeve to try to wipe off fingerprints in and around the truck.

Beach ran toward home, but realized as he got close that he was covered in blood. He stripped to his underwear, wiped the blood off his body as best as he could, then burned the clothes in a railroad car that was parked on the tracks. He ran the rest of the way home, washed the remaining blood off, and went to sleep trying to convince himself that it didn't really happen.

That was, more or less, the story Beach told Louisiana officers multiple times over the course of several different interviews. It matched enough of the details that the Montana authorities believed him and charged him with the murder. Even with the bungled crime scene, the confession was enough for a jury to convict him. He was sentenced to 100 years with no chance of parole,

that later. Second, they argued that the group of girls actually murdered Nees, and they found multiple new witnesses to "prove" it.

The group of girls were three girls named Sissy Atkinson, Maude Grayhawk and JoAnn Todd (Jackson at the time). Centurion produced an eyewitness in 2004 who claimed that he saw Kimberly's murder. The witness, Calvin Lester, said that he was 10 years old at the time and he had seen a group of girls at the train bridge kicking another girl who was on the ground. Lester said that Maude Grayhawk was one of the attackers.

Roosevelt County investigators brought Maude in for an interview in 2004. She said that she and several other people had been partying at the bridge earlier on the night of Kimberly's murder but had left by 10:00 p.m. She denied that she had anything to do with Kim's death, and wouldn't budge from the story even when investigators told her about an eyewitness.

When investigators went back to Lester after Maude's interview, he admitted that he made the entire thing up and never saw Kim's murder.

Centurion found another witness by the name of Richard Holen who claimed to have seen Nees' truck at the train bridge the night of the murder. Holen said that there were five people in the truck. During one statement, he said that all five were female. During a later statement, he said that it was actually a man sitting by the passenger door. Holen's story changed a little with each telling. There was also another truck with Kimberly's truck, apparently.

Not to cast aspersions on anybody, but Holen's story seemed to be whatever Centurion needed it to be at that particular time. Coincidence, I'm sure.

Centurion found another witness named Carl Four Star who worked with Sissy Atkinson in 1985. Four Star overheard Atkinson telling another co-worker that Atkinson was there on the night Kim was murdered. Then she made a kicking motion to indicate that she was in on it. Four Star overheard this from about 25 feet away, even though they worked in a factory and other workers claimed that the ventilation fans were so loud you had to yell for the person next to you to hear. Just for good measure, Four Star said Atkinson walked up to him later in the day and told him that she had gotten away with the perfect murder. Just in case she hadn't incriminated herself thoroughly enough already, I guess. Four Star didn't tell anybody about this until Centurion showed up at his mother's house looking for witnesses more than 15 years later.

Centurion also found assorted witnesses who claimed to have heard various incriminating statements by Atkinson, Grayhawk and Todd over the years. Each witness had a weirder backstory than the last and none of it was very convincing. I'm not going to waste your time with the details. Your time is too important for that.

The one significant witness Centurion managed to find was Steffanie Eagle Boy. Out of everybody, she told a story that resonated. And she seemed the least like she was making it up. Eagle Boy was 10 years old and lived near the Train Bridge in Poplar in 1979. She liked to sit out on a rock overlooking the train bridge with her cousin, Joel Sparvier. One night in 1979, Eagle Boy and Sparvier were sitting on the rock when she saw two pick-ups pull onto the train bridge. A group of girls got out and then Eagle Boy heard about 10 to 20 minutes of "horrific screaming" and girls saying "get her" and "kick the bitch." Then it got quiet and a police car arrived with its emergency lights on. The cop car shut off all of its lights, and Eagle Boy heard some whispering and then some clanking as if somebody was digging. Both pickups and the cop car then drove away.

I don't think Eagle Boy was lying, I just don't think she saw the Kimberly Nees murder. Kim's truck stayed at the scene, so it wouldn't make sense that all three vehicles left. Kim wasn't buried and none of the investigators saw anything to suggest other evidence was either. And, unbeknownst to Eagle Boy, Sparvier actually testfied at the original trial, which was only 5 years after the murder not 25 years later like Eagle Boy's story was. Sparvier didn't see any of the things Eagle Boy described.

Whatever Eagle Boy saw probably fell short of a murder. Murders are rare and newsworthy on the reservation. But whatever she saw certainly sounds like a crime. Just not the particular crime we are trying to solve here. It sounds like the train bridge was an interesting place in the summer of 1979.

I promised you two governors, so now seems like a good time to introduce Montana Governor Steve Bullock into the story. Bullock was the Attorney General at the time when Beach presented all of this information in an appeal. As Attorney General, it was Bullock's job to argue that Beach was guilty and belonged in prison. He did such a good job that, after a lower court released him for a few months, Beach was ultimately sent back to prison to finish his term.

That was 2011, but by 2013 Bullock was the Governor of Montana. Among his new duties was to consider requests for clemency. The most high profile request to hit his desk was that of Barry Beach. And between the *Dateline* specials and some questionably fact-checked reporting in the state's newspapers, public opinion had swung strongly behind Beach. A sizable chunk of Bullock's electorate was convinced that Beach was innocent and should be freed immediately. The smart move, politically, would have been to grant him clemency and release him. But since Bullock was the one who kept Beach in jail by arguing in public documents that Beach was absolutely guilty of the murder, he would make himself look like an idiot or a liar to publicly proclaim Beach innocent and grant him clemency.

You don't get as far as Bullock has politically without dodging a few dog turds, so he found a brilliant way of stepping around the problem. The United States Supreme Court came out with an opinion that argued strongly against sentences of life without parole for minors. That wasn't technically Beach's sentence, but unless he lived to be 121 years old, it was essentially the same thing. Bullock argued that Beach's sentence was unfair in light of the Supreme Court decision, that Beach was a changed man and that Beach had served a fair sentence for the murder. Governor Bullock managed to release Beach without having to call Attorney General Bullock an idiot or a liar.

We won't be so lucky in our quest. No easy way out for us. We're here to solve a murder. We need to figure out if Beach killed Nees. If he didn't, we need to figure out who did.

The first question is going to boil down to what we think of the confession. Off the top, I don't believe it was coerced. Beach was advised of his Miranda rights ten times. He wasn't beaten or threatened. He was fed and rested and treated with common courtesy. I know that Sodium Pentothal existed and was occasionally used back then, but I don't believe they secretly dosed Beach's milkshake like he claimed. I don't even think Sodium Pentothal works the way Beach described. I think Beach's confession was voluntary. But that doesn't necessarily make it true. Let's see how it holds up to the facts in the case.

The start of the story, where Beach ruined the transmission then physically assaulted his car, is backed up by two independent witnesses. The other guys who were at the beach with him corroborated the story and said that Beach was indeed very pissed off. So we are off to a good start as far as Beach telling the truth. But nothing that happened out at Sandy Beach is the least bit relevant to Kimberly's murder, so let's move on.

The part of the story where Beach goes home and takes a nap isn't backed up by witnesses or evidence, but it isn't important to the story and I don't think we should waste time trying to parse whether or not it is true. We've got enough to deal with when we get to the substance of the story.

Beach said that he walked into town and saw Kimberly sitting alone in her truck but talking to somebody in another vehicle. He didn't know the time, but said it was after dark. Beach described a spot where independent witnesses saw Nees. That may have been common knowledge around town by the time Beach made his confession. Beach didn't remember who Kim was talking to, but police never found any witnesses who said they had talked to Kim in her truck at the Exxon that night. We'll call this part of the confession plausible and consistent enough with the known facts, but also note that it doesn't contain any information that wasn't publicly available at the time.

Beach asked Kim if she knew where her sister Pam was, then asked Kim if he could ride around with her. This is where some Beach supporters start to call B.S. Kim was the valedictorian and Beach was a troublemaker. They also allege that Kim thought Beach was an asshole and wouldn't have let him ride with her. Obviously I don't know anybody involved with this, but I'm still calling it plausible. She seemed to be pissed off about her boyfriend going to the bar without her, and she had just driven around with another guy the night before. Teenagers are known to act differently alone than they might in their normal social circles, and maybe Kim was looking for somebody to talk to, even if she did think Beach was an asshole. Plus, if we're being honest, Beach was a very handsome kid and that's the kind of thing that might convince a young girl to overlook some basic personality defects. We might differ on this one, but I'm calling it plausible.

Nobody saw Beach and Kim together so obviously we have no way to corroborate the events that Beach described leading up to the assault. The idea of two kids smoking a joint and talking about life doesn't seem out of the ordinary. And the story of a teenage boy trying to push himself sexually on a girl who wasn't interested is a cliché in any era, unfortunately. We have no way to know if it's true, but I see nothing on the surface that says it's false either.

The part where Beach beats Kim in the head with a crescent wrench in the cab of the truck was the foundation of his conviction. It explains so much about the inside of the cab. It's a small enough weapon to use in a confined space, it's hard and heavy enough to crack a skull, and it matched at least some of Kim's injuries. Forensically, it was a winner. It would explain the gouges and embedded hair in the ceiling and steering wheel, too. Plus, Kim's father had already said that a 12-inch crescent wrench was missing from the truck.

Therein lies one issue with that part of the story. Kim's father said the wrench was in the toolbox and he couldn't think of a reason why it would be in the cab of the truck. Beach said he grabbed it from the floorboard. There are a hundred reasons that the wrench could have made it from the toolbox to the floorboard without Kim's father's knowledge. He hadn't driven the truck in at least a week. But it is a curious discrepancy. Police insisted that only the real killer would have known that a crescent wrench was used, but I'm not super confident that small details like that didn't leak out around town over the course of the investigation. It's a small town and we've already mentioned Governor Racicot's thoughts on the investigation several times.

Overall, I'd say that the details about what happened inside the cab make me believe Beach more than they make me doubt him. But they certainly aren't conclusive one way or the other.

Now onto where the attack moved outside of the truck. Beach said that Kim got out of the driver's door and tried to escape, but he made it out the passenger side and around in time to pin her against the driver's side. It's not the simplest thing to accept, but I'll buy it. Kim would have been severely injured, disoriented and scared. Maybe she wasn't moving too fast. Beach then said that he tried to kiss her, but she scratched him. That part is weird, but not unheard of. And Beach likes to claim now that he had no scratch marks the following day, but it doesn't sound like anybody really checked him out to verify that.

Beach said that he then grabbed a tire iron from the back of the truck and hit Kim in the head. She tried to run off, so he tackled her a short distance from the rear passenger tire and finished her off with the tire iron. These were the details that doomed him. Investigators had previously noted the blood spot where Beach was describing. That is not the kind of minute detail I would expect to be salacious enough to make it through the small town grapevine even if it was leaked. And the tire iron Beach described matched Kim's injuries as well. So much so that Dr. Pfaff was comfortable saying the crescent wrench and tire iron combined could have caused all of Kim's injuries.

Those details are pretty damn convincing. If he was guessing, how did he guess a murder weapon that fit the injuries perfectly and the exact location where Kim left a visible blood spot? Plus, Kim's father said that there was a tire iron in the back of the truck. I would almost call this thing solved except for a couple of minor quibbles. Kim's father said that the truck had two tire irons in the tool box, one "L" shaped and one cross-shaped. But Pam Nees, who also occasionally drove the truck, told investigators that there was only a cross-shaped one. Even on the truck I drove, I know my dad would have been a far better authority on what types of tools were in the truck than I would have been as a teenager. But if Pam Nees was right, the cross-shaped tire iron wouldn't match the injuries. Also, Kim's father said that the tire iron was kept in the toolbox and Beach didn't mention anything about opening a toolbox.

Like I said, both of those things are minor quibbles. But I think we should probably keep them in mind when we weigh this thing out.

Beach said that he found a garbage bag in the back of Kim's truck and tried to stuff her in it to drag her to the river. The state contends that such a setup would be consistent with the peculiar drag marks at the scene. Beach's supporters insist that Kim didn't have any trash bags in her truck and that one wouldn't have stayed intact on that long of a drag. I don't have an opinion either way. I'm not enough of an expert on drag marks to say for certain and I'd raise an eyebrow at anybody who claimed they were. Raise an eyebrow to their face. To you, behind their back, I'd quietly call that person a quack.

I could tell earlier you were bothered by part of Beach's story. That part where he claimed to have checked Kim's pulse. It was faint, and then it stopped. He got that from a movie or TV show didn't he? He just said it because it sounds like something you are supposed to do when somebody is dying. Watch an EMT try to find a faint pulse. That's not easy for real medical people to do, let alone a stoned teenager with no training. I'm with you on this one. It doesn't matter in the grand scheme of the overall story, but I'm calling nonsense on this part. He didn't check her pulse. And if he tried, he definitely couldn't tell when it stopped.

Beach said that after he pushed Kim's body into the river he retrieved the wrench, the tire iron, the keys and Kim's jacket and threw them into the river as well. Not all in one trip, from the sounds of his description either. As we mentioned before, it was 80 yards from the truck to the river bank. Not the kind of trip you want to make more than you have to in the haste of cleaning a murder scene. And what is the point of throwing the keys in the river? I'm not saying it didn't happen, but this part of the story makes me believe it a little less. Obviously the keys were missing so somebody disposed of them, but Beach doesn't give a real satisfying explanation why. As we mentioned in a previous chapter, criminals do perplexing things sometimes and you can drive yourself nutty trying to understand why.

Beach's supporters claim that his description didn't match Kim's actual clothing, but that part of the confession seemed pretty ambiguous and confusing to me. The court acknowledged at least one discrepancy in the clothing description, so we should probably recognize that there was at least one.

Detectives asked a couple of different times about Kim's purse. Beach said that he saw it in the cab of the truck and then later said that he thought he saw it outside of the passenger side door. But he didn't say anything about the sweater. Beach's supporters insist that the sweater was folded neatly. I have my doubts from the crime scene photo. But regardless, Beach didn't say anything about a sweater.

I'm going to criticize the detectives a little bit on this one, and by that I mean point out a serious flaw in my own interviews that is more fun to criticize in others. The detectives spoke as much as Beach did on the transcript I read. They seemed to ask questions quickly and directly. They interrupted Beach's train of thought for clarifying details rather than coming back for them after he finished the thought. It isn't an ideal way to interview suspects. But man, I've been there. Interviews are so freaking frustrating sometimes. People suck so bad at telling stories. They jump all over the place. They leave out important details and then remember them out of nowhere later. They rely exclusively on pronouns even in a story that has a dozen people, then they make no attempt to distinguish who the pronoun is supposed to be. They give you either no context or way too much context. They ramble about insignificant nonsense then gloss over the actual crime. It is a pain in the ass to listen to an actual confession. And it is so tempting to cut them off and ask direct questions for the details you need.

But memory is a weird thing. Not everybody catches the same details. And you never know what details are going to register with somebody who was in the middle of a stressful situation, such as a murder. As tempting as it is to cut them off and ask for clarifying details like the time of day, the clothing that a victim was wearing or the location of a key piece of evidence, there is a real possibility that they won't remember. Which won't stop them from guessing just to make you happy. So then you have wrong details in a genuine confession. And they are pulled away from whatever thread of a story they were working on. The next time you find yourself getting a confession out of a murderer, remember to shut up and let them tell their story. In their own disjointed, winding and convoluted way they will tell you most of the details that stuck with them. And you can try to ask some follow up questions when they are done if you need to flush out more information. Just be careful they don't guess at key facts to make you happy.

But you and I aren't going to be taking confessions in this book. That part has already been done for us. And since those poor Louisiana detectives had already heard this story from Beach multiple times, we can forgive them for running out of patience.

The biggest issue I have with Beach's confession is that he claimed to have choked Kim, but the autopsy report didn't describe any strangulation injuries. Maybe he didn't choke her long enough or hard enough to leave a mark or fracture the hyoid, but I don't like that part of the confession. I wish he hadn't said it, or I wish the medical examiner had found something to substantiate it.

With that in mind, we can acknowledge that Beach did not get everything exactly right in his confession but still recognize that it is really damn close. Close enough to be believable. Absent a better suspect, we'd probably be fine saying he did it and calling this one solved. But let's go over the other suspects one more time before we close the book on this.

Investigators heard the rumors about a group of girls early in the investigation. The roster of who exactly was among that group has been fluid over the years, depending on who was telling the story, but by 2004 Centurion Ministries settled on Sissy Atkinson, Maude Grayhawk and JoAnn Todd. Not so much because they figured prominently into the earlier rumors, but because they were able to uncover some incriminating "evidence" against those three. And you are supposed to infer skepticism from those quotation marks. It was mostly sketchy second-hand confessions overheard under the influence of drugs or alcohol.

JoAnn Todd was actually a witness in Beach's first trial. A defense witness at that. Beach's attorney didn't bring up the group of girls or accuse Todd of anything. He was actually trying to get Todd to say that she had heard a completely unrelated rumor about Kim's murder. But Todd's memory on the stand differed from what she had told the FBI during the early days of the investigation. That's the trouble with rumors. They are hard enough to keep straight at the time and nearly impossible four years after the fact.

I don't think a group of girls killed Kim. All of the rumors allege that a group of girls lured her to the river and then kicked and beat her to death. But the autopsy didn't show those types of injuries. The autopsy shows that Kim was hit in the head repeatedly with a weapon or weapons and that she tried to protect herself with her hands and arms. A group beating would have left a lot of lesser injuries to the body that weren't present on Kim.

There is one really odd thing about the group of girls theory that I can't explain away and it would be irresponsible of me not to talk about it. You've probably already noticed it. Remember when I mentioned earlier about the Poplar Police Department officer who kicked in the judge's door to use the restroom? I'm sure you probably already caught that his last name was Grayhawk. As in Maude Grayhawk's father.

Maybe Officer Grayhawk was telling the truth about his motives, but that is one of the damndest coincidences I've ever heard of. He commits a burglary to use the restroom and contaminates evidence in the process, and his daughter is accused of the crime years later. I don't know what to make of this information. But the Poplar Police Department was a minor player in the investigation and I have a hard time believing that they would have been trusted with any meaningful evidence. Regardless of Officer Grayhawk's motives, I just don't think he would have been able to alter the course of the investigation with anything he did in the judge's chambers that night. At least that's what I'm telling myself to keep this story on track.

Which brings us to the final suspect, Greg Norgaard.

I know it's a cliché at this point, but there is a reason we always look at the boyfriend/spouse/significant other. Statistically, it's such a great place to start. And not to dive too deep into the psychology of the attacker, which I am always skeptical of, but that was an excessively violent attack. Kim would have died from a lot less. Whenever I see violence like that, I tend to think it's personal. It's hard to generate that much hate for a stranger or a casual acquaintance. That feels like a domestic violence thing.

The relationship problems between Norgaard and Kim in the two days leading up to her murder are a giant red flag. Motive isn't everything in an investigation, but it's something. Unless you subscribe to the group of jealous girls theory, nobody else really had a motive to kill her.

And as far as alibis go, Norgaard had about as poor of one as you can have when you are the prime suspect in a murder investigation. He left the bar and was out looking for the victim? Alone? And nobody could definitively say when he got home? That's not an alibi at all.

The payphone calls he made after leaving the bar are open to interpretation. On one hand, calling the victim's house to talk to her mother is a bad idea if you are planning on killing her later. But if the killing was truly a crime of passion and not planned, then maybe calling home and finding that she wasn't there just enraged him further. And calling the ex-girlfriend because he wanted to make Kim jealous just seems like classic drunk dialing. What a time to be alive. Whatever you said while you were drunk was lost forever in the hangover. There was no text message paper trail to haunt you the next day.

Don't judge me for this because I know it sounds really twisted. Don't read it out loud please. But I think the fact that Kim was not sexually assaulted points more toward the Norgaard theory than it does the Beach theory. If we believe Beach's confession, the entire thing blew up because he was trying to get Kim to have sex with him. And he still tried to kiss her against the truck while she was bleeding and screaming. Wouldn't we kind of expect him to sexually assault her? But no such thing showed up in the autopsy. If we think that Norgaard did it, we think he did it in a jealous rage. We wouldn't necessarily expect to see a sexual assault under those conditions.

Investigators tried their best to link Norgaard to the crime but couldn't find anything. Sometimes that happens because the person is innocent and sometimes it happens because investigators can't find the evidence. So which scenario should we go with?

It's surprisingly close for me. I was somewhat familiar with this case coming in because I had read the media reports. I was certain Beach had committed the murder and I would get irritated with my own mother when she suggested otherwise. Sorry mom.

I am less certain after reviewing the case, but I still think Beach probably did it. The confession was pretty close and nothing he got wrong is a real dealbreaker for me. And he was, as has been pointed out a couple of times by a couple of different sources, widely regarded as an asshole in 1979. He threatened to kill his stepmother. His own father told police that he was absolutely capable of murder. Then after he got out of jail, Beach was jailed on a probation violation less than a year later, accused of stalking a woman. The charge was dropped and he was released, but there was at least enough evidence to charge him in the first place.

Norgaard seems to have gone on to live a normal life. He eventually became the mayor of Poplar. I'm not so naive as to think that an elected official is above a heinous act like this, but Norgaard's life didn't shake out the way I would expect from somebody who committed a brutal murder in his early twenties. Even if he had a motive to do it and his alibi is nonexistent, I don't think it was him.

Shall we go with Beach on this one? Good, glad that's settled.

Hae Min Lee

I did not listen to the *Serial* podcast until almost five years after it came out. It was released around the same time as the *Making a Murderer* documentary and I lumped it into the same category. That was a mistake. *Serial* isn't the same species as *Making a Murderer*, and the medium has nothing to do with it. *Making a Murderer* was so manipulative and dishonest in the way it presented the facts of Teresa Halbach's murder that I refused to watch the second season or anything else by its creators. They wanted Steven Avery to be innocent for the sake of their show and when it became apparent that he wasn't, they basically lied through a series of omissions and misrepresentations. *Serial* host Sarah Koenig wanted the subject of her story to be innocent as well, and admitted as much during the course of the show, but never let that cloud her journalistic responsibility to tell the truth. Koenig and her producers did a really in-depth investigation, which included interviewing witnesses, consulting experts and recreating scenarios. They did it responsibly, with a real attention to detail. Then they laid all of the facts bare before their listeners, with no thought as to whether or not those facts supported the story they hoped was true. That's real journalism. And it was entertaining to boot. *Serial* was everything we could hope for when we are solving murders.

All that said, I don't agree with Koenig's conclusion and I don't think you will either.

Of course, we haven't agreed on everything so far. Which surprises me. We're both intelligent, reasonable, beautiful people, so I kind of assumed we'd agree on everything. But somehow we don't. We can look at the exact same facts and somehow come to different conclusions. Maybe you're right or maybe I am right but, either way, somehow we remain friends. What a strange situation that we are able to appreciate and respect the opinions of friends with whom we disagree. Didn't they pass a law in 2008 that we have to shout at and belittle anybody who challenges our beliefs? Are we going to jail for all of this civility? Surely they would have to give us some credit for all of these murders we solved. That has to count for something, right?

Just to be sure, we'll do an especially good job on this one.

Our sources on this case are going to be *Serial* and a collection of court transcripts and police reports compiled at adnansyedwiki.com, a website devoted to the investigation. I want to thank both for doing such a comprehensive job of assembling and presenting information on the case.

I swear I am not copying and pasting this from the Kimberly Nees story, but Hae Min Lee was a beautiful and smart teenager who was destined to do great things with her life. She was a senior at Woodlawn High School in Baltimore, Maryland, in January of 1999. She was in the magnet program, which was an accelerated academic program with a lot of advanced placement classes. She was a Korean-American and her circle of friends in the magnet program appeared to be a real melting pot of ethnicities and cultures. She played field hockey and lacrosse, managed the wrestling team and was still able to get good grades. She was helpful around the house, worked a part-time job and was pretty much the ideal of what anybody would want in a daughter.

At about 6:00 p.m. on January 13, 1999, Baltimore County Police Officer Scott Adcock was called to a home in Baltimore for a report of a missing person. Young Lee reported that his sister, Hae Lee, was missing. She was supposed to pick up her cousin from kindergarten after school that day, but never did. Nobody in the family had seen Hae since she went to school that morning and she had never done anything like that before.

This type of call is pretty common in law enforcement and I imagine especially so in a city the size of Baltimore. Teenagers run away all the time. And no matter how many times it's happened, parents and family members will still insist that the runaway has never done that kind of thing before. Most police are jaded to it and skeptical when they get a report of a missing teenager. They are almost always runaways who come home on their own when they are ready.

The form that Officer Adcock used to take the report had two boxes for him to check, depending on the circumstances: one for a missing person and one for a runaway. Officer Adcock chose to check the missing person box. Hae was only a few hours overdue and she was 18 years old, technically an adult. But something about Hae's home and family made Adcock understand immediately that she was not the type of kid to just run away. That detail really stuck with me. Not that it should matter, but it seems like Hae was a really good kid from a really good family.

In addition to Hae's family, Officer Adcock also spoke to two witnesses who knew Hae from school. A girl named Aisha confirmed that Hae had been in school that day. Aisha saw Hae there at about 2:15 p.m. A boy named Adnan Syed also saw Hae in school that day. He was supposed to get a ride from her after school, but didn't because he got held up late.

I don't like to spoil the story this early, but Syed was eventually convicted of Hae's murder. You probably already know that from the media coverage, and you definitely figured it out when you saw that one of our sources was adnansyedwiki.com, so I didn't want to insult your intelligence by pretending that you don't already know how this ends. Just act surprised for me when we get to that point of the story, please.

Officer Adcock talked with Hae's boss at Lenscrafters and learned that she had not been to work on January

13. Officer Adcock also learned that Hae's 1998 Nissan Sentra was missing. Over the next couple of weeks, officers checked the local hospitals, hotels, and public parking lots looking for Hae or her car, but had no luck. By February 6, things were looking bleak and the police brought in a search dog to check the area around the school. Again, there was no sign of Hae.

Police briefly entertained the notion that Hae might have run off to California to live with her father. A couple of witnesses said she had talked about California before and a couple others also said that she recently had had some disagreements with her mother about her curfew and other teenage problems. The police dismissed the theory when it became apparent that Hae's arguments with her mother were very minor and that she never had any real plans to go to California.

Stop me if you've heard this line before, but police quickly turned their attention to Hae's boyfriend, Don. Don worked at Lenscrafters with Hae and they had been dating for about two weeks. He was a few years older than Hae and out of school. Police didn't reach him for the first time until about 1:30 a.m. the morning after Hae's disappearance. Don told Officer Adcock that he did not know where Hae was and hadn't spoken to her since January 12.

Police did a follow up interview with Don on January 22. Again Don said that he last saw Hae on January 12. She was in good spirits and did not give any indication that she intended to run away. Don said that Hae was at his house until about 10:30 p.m. that evening, and that they spoke on the phone after she got home until about 3:00 a.m.

Don told police he worked at Lenscrafters on January 13 until about 6:00 p.m. He normally worked at Lenscrafters in the Owings Mill Mall, where Hae also worked, but on that particular day he was covering for a friend at the Hunt Valley Mall. When he arrived home at about 7:00 p.m., he was told by his father to call the Owings Mill Lenscrafters because Hae was missing.

Don's boss verified that Don had been working until 6:00 p.m. on January 13, but since Don's boss was also his mother, they did not rule him out as a suspect completely until they verified the rest of the details of his story. Eventually they concluded that he was telling the truth and could not have been anywhere near the school where Hae was last seen.

Police then turned their attention to Syed.

On January 25, a Baltimore County Detective talked to Syed on the phone. Syed claimed that he had been in class with Hae on January 13 from 12:50 until 2:15 p.m. He went to track practice after school, never saw Hae and had no idea what had happened to her. Syed also told the detective that he used to date Hae, but they broke up in December of 1998. Syed said he was from a Muslim family and his parents did not allow him to date, so the relationship had been kept secret from his family.

As they were reviewing their investigative files, detectives realized they had actually already spoken to

Syed on the night of the initial report. He said at that time he was supposed to get a ride from Hae after school, but never did. Syed did not mention this in the phone call with detectives on January 25, so they called him back on February 1. This time Syed said Hae would not have been waiting to give him a ride on the day she went missing because Syed had his own car. Detectives arranged a face-to-face interview with Syed and his parents for February 10, but it was postponed after the tragic discovery of Hae's body on February 9.

Hae was discovered in a shallow grave in a place called Leakin Park by a Coppin State University janitor. The man was on his way to work and discovered Hae's body when he stopped to relieve himself.

Leakin Park is a 300 acre park that the *Baltimore Sun* once referred to as "the city's largest unregistered graveyard." According to a July 5, 1997 *Sun* story, at least 56 dead bodies were found in the park between 1968 and 1997. The same story called it "an urban forest… where children discover skeletons and city workers find bullet-riddled corpses draped over guardrails."

Not to tell people how to do their jobs or anything, but it sounds like Leakin Park might be the first place you want to look for a missing person in Baltimore.

Detectives and crime scene techs responded and searched the area. As is usually the case when a body is discovered in a public place, it was hard to tell what items were related to Hae's death and what items were unrelated debris that just happened to be in the way.

Officers recovered a half-full pint of liquor, a section of clothesline, 19 fired cartridge cases, a rolled condom, a condom wrapper and several Blockbuster video cases in the general area where Hae was found. I'm trying really hard to piece together a story where all of those items fit, but it isn't easy. A laundry target shooting party gone awry? A clandestine VHS porno theater in the woods? The world's worst birthday clown rehearsing in the park? I can't really make anything fit. Police couldn't either and didn't find a connection between any of those things and Hae's death.

Dr. Marlon Aquino performed an autopsy the following day and determined that Hae had been murdered by strangulation. He noted hemorrhaging and contusions on the neck muscles along with a dislocated hyoid bone and petechial hemorrhaging in the eyes, all consistent with strangulation. There was no sign that a ligature was used, and the marks were consistent with a manual strangulation.

Dr. Aquino also noted blunt force injuries to the back and right side of Hae's head. There was some bleeding between the scalp and the skull, but no skull fractures and no bleeding within the skull.

And since I can't think of a delicate or more clinical way to describe this, I'll just quote Dr. Aquino's report: "The white jacket the decedent was wearing was unbuttoned along its anterior middle opening; the skirt and bra were partly pulled up, exposing both breasts onto which wet soil was adherent. The pantyhose had prominent defects on the knees. The skirt was pulled up at the level of the buttocks." Dr. Aquino swabbed Hae's intimate parts but did not find any male bodily fluids or any other sign of sexual abuse.

Sorry. I wish we could have skipped that part altogether, but I think it will matter to us later on.

Hae's family and friends confirmed the clothes Hae's body was discovered in were the same clothes she had worn to school the day she was reported missing. Between that, the state of decomposition and the fact that nobody had seen her since school that day, police determined that Hae was probably killed on January 13.

There were essentially two rounds of interviews done with Hae's friends and schoolmates. The first round was done by Baltimore County Police after she was reported missing. The second round was done by the Baltimore City Police Department after her body was found. Two of Baltimore County's interviews were within a day or two of Hae's disappearance and it's reasonable to think that a person would remember even mundane details after only a day or two. The rest of the interviews took place weeks or months after Hae was last seen. Think of a casual acquaintance from work or school. Now pick a random day about a month ago. Do you remember what time you last saw them that day? Do you remember what they were wearing? Do you remember anything about their demeanor?

That's a little bit unfair because you would surely remember a little more if that person had gone missing the next day. But even then, you aren't going to be nearly as accurate as you would have been the next day. Just keep that in mind while we try to piece together this timeline, because it doesn't exactly fit.

As we already mentioned, Hae's friend Aisha told Officer Adcock on January 14 that she last saw Hae at about 2:15 p.m. the previous day, which was the end of their school day. Syed said that Hae was in school, but did not give a specific time when he last saw her.

Two weeks after she went missing, police talked to a friend of Hae's by the name of Debbie. Debbie said that she last saw Hae in school at about 3:00 p.m. on January 13. Hae was by herself and near the gym. She told Debbie that she was going to meet her boyfriend Don at the mall.

Police wanted to zero in on Don and Syed right away, but another suspect inserted himself into the investigation and took up a few days of their time. The Coppin State janitor who discovered Hae's body turned out to have a bit of a past. First of all, he had to relieve himself in the park because he'd had himself a couple of lunch beers at home. I hate to judge, but lunch beers have a strong correlation to poor decision making in life. I know there was a time when men in suits would close important business deals over afternoon steaks and cocktails, but that's a far cry from lunch beers. Lunch beers are almost always cheap tallboys, in a can, and consumed alone and in secret over a lunch of saltine crackers. I'm not suggesting that every person who indulges in a tall Bud Light on their lunch break is a killer, but if you and I are working on an unsolved homicide and a key witness mentions lunch beer, we will be paying very close attention to them until we can rule them out.

The janitor also had a history of indecent exposure charges around the Baltimore area. Again, I'm not saying every sexual deviant is a murderer, but when a key witness in an unsolved homicide turns out to be a sexual deviant, they need to be investigated thoroughly. Especially in light of what we already noted about Hae's clothing.

The janitor cooperated fully with the investigation and gave multiple interviews, including two polygraphs. He failed one, of course, but one out of two isn't bad. Police ultimately determined that the janitor was not involved in the murder, but not before wasting a lot of time and resources running down alibi witnesses and workplace records.

A word about the polygraph, just in case you get hung up on the failed one. The polygraph is an amazing investigative tool for obtaining a confession, but it isn't actually all that good at detecting lies. It's a scary proposition to lie to a "lie detector," so a lot of people will just confess rather than get caught by the machine. Other people will confess after the polygraph operator tells them that the machine knows they are lying. A really skilled polygraph operator can tell a lot about a person from a polygraph. They can tell what questions are causing a physiological response. They can tell what topics a person is trying to avoid. They can tell when somebody is pulling shenanigans to try to cheat the machine. But they can't really tell if a person is lying. They can make an educated guess, but it's still just a guess. There is a reason that polygraph results aren't admissible in court.

On the surface, it seems ridiculous to think that the janitor would have had anything to do with the murder. There would be no sensible reason for him to alert police to the body if he was the murderer. But criminals are weird and do a lot of really weird things sometimes. I'm not sure which blowhard popularized the theory that all criminals return to the scene of the crime, because that's not true at all, but I will admit that many criminals do things that only make sense to them. And while exposing yourself to strangers isn't the same thing as killing another person, it's a step in that direction. It might not be as violent, but it's in the same neighborhood as rape. And rape is on the same street as murder.

Fortunately, the Baltimore Police Department did all of the hard work on the janitor and confirmed his alibi for us. That would have been really tough for us to do after so much time has passed, and he is exactly the type of oddball red herring that could have really derailed our entire investigation.

With the janitor off their list, investigators returned their attention to where it was before the discovery of Hae's body: Adnan Syed.

On the afternoon of February 12, Baltimore Police Detective Darryl Massey received a call from an anonymous male who said that police should focus on Syed as a suspect in Hae's murder. The caller said that Syed and Hae had spent time together in Leakin Park before and that Hae had broken up with Syed about a week before she went missing. The anonymous male called back a second time, six minutes later. This time he said that about a year before the murder Syed told a mutual acquaintance of theirs that if he ever hurt his girlfriend he would drive her car into the lake. Police couldn't identify the anonymous male, but did speak to the mutual acquaintance, who did not remember any such conversation with Syed. And ultimately her car wasn't in a lake, so take that for what it's worth.

Young Barney Doyle was still quite a few years away from getting his first cell phone at the time, but it was not unheard of for a teenager to have a cell phone in 1999. Most kids didn't, but some did. Hae didn't, but Syed did. Investigators subpoenaed records from Syed's phone and found that among the calls on January 13 was one to a girl by the name of Jennifer.

Detectives met with Jennifer on the night of February 26, and she said that she did not know anything about Hae's murder. She came back the following day with an attorney, however, and told a much different story.

Jennifer told police that on the morning of January 13 she was working at her job as a lifeguard. Sometime between 10:00 a.m. and noon, she called her friend Jay Wilds to see if he wanted to hang out when she got off work. That may or may not have been code for "smoke weed" because Wilds was a small-time weed dealer. Jennifer offered to pick Wilds up when she got off of work, but Wilds said he had a ride and would meet her at her house. It should be noted, however, that Jay did not own a car, which was why Jennifer offered him a ride in the first place.

Jennifer got home around 1:00 p.m. and Wilds came over sometime before 2:00 p.m. They played video games for a while and Wilds told Jennifer he was waiting for a phone call. Wilds had a cell phone with him, but Jennifer couldn't remember if he said who the phone or the car he was driving belonged to. But at some point later that day, Wilds told Jennifer the car belonged to Syed. Jennifer did not know Syed very well, as evidenced by the fact that she called him Adnar instead of Adnan throughout her interview.

Wilds got a phone call sometime between 2:30 p.m. and 4:15 p.m., then left Jennifer's house. Jennifer thought Wilds was acting nervous but didn't ask him about it. She was supposed to meet up with him later that night and figured she would ask him about his strange behavior then.

Jennifer ran some errands then returned to find a voice message from Wilds on her answering machine. Wilds was asking Jennifer to pick him up from the park later that evening, but his instructions weren't clear so she tried calling him back. Syed answered the phone and told Jennifer that Wilds would call when he was ready for a ride.

She called Syed's cell phone. How did she have the number, you might be wondering? Pagers. Everybody in this story had a pager. Almost nobody had pagers where I lived back then, but my editor says they were all the rage with teenagers in 1999 in Southern California. Apparently in Baltimore too. I assumed only drug dealers and police officers carried pagers, but you learn something new everyday. At any rate, Wilds apparently paged Jennifer with Syed's cell phone number at some point.

Sometime between 8:00 p.m. and 8:30 p.m., Jennifer got a page from Wilds telling her to meet him at the Westview Mall. She was there waiting for about fifteen minutes before Jay and Syed arrived in Syed's car. They exchanged brief pleasantries before Wilds got into Jennifer's car and they drove off.

Wilds told Jennifer he had something to tell her, but that she had to swear to keep it a secret. She agreed, and Wilds told her that Syed had killed Hae that afternoon. Wilds said Hae broke Syed's heart so Syed strangled her to death.

This was a huge break in the case for the Baltimore Police Department. The suspect she blamed was one they were already investigating, the motive she described was simple and logical, and her description of the crime matched the evidence (as far as the strangling). But it was a third-hand account, and Jennifer couldn't give them anything to substantiate what she was saying. She claimed that Wilds ditched his clothing and some shovels in various trash cans, but too much time had passed for them to be recovered. Phone and pager logs could corroborate that some of the conversations she described happened, but they couldn't verify what was actually said. Jennifer pointed them in a promising direction, but they had a lot of work to do before they could determine if it was the truth.

Shortly after midnight on February 28, detectives interviewed Wilds. Wilds said Syed had called him on the morning of January 13, and then the two of them went to the Westview Mall to shop for a birthday present for Wilds' girlfriend. While they were shopping, Syed asked Wilds to take his car and phone. Wilds was then supposed to pick up Syed when he called that afternoon.

Syed and Wilds were talking about girls and Syed said that he couldn't believe what Hae had done to him. Syed said that Hae broke his heart and that he was going to kill her.

Wilds claimed that Syed said, "I'm going to do it. I'm going to kill that bitch."

Wilds told detectives he did not believe Syed was actually going to kill Hae, but he dropped Syed back off at school and agreed to pick him up when Syed called. Wilds was playing video games with Jennifer's younger brother when Syed called the cell phone at about 3:40 p.m. and told Wilds to meet him at a spot on Edmondson Avenue.

Wilds arrived to find Syed driving Hae's car. Syed was wearing red gloves and Wilds asked why. Syed said he killed Hae, then opened the trunk and showed Wilds the body. Wilds correctly described for detectives the clothes that Hae had been wearing.

The two men argued for a few minutes on the side of the road, then Syed told Wilds to follow him. They drove the two vehicles to a park-and-ride on Route 70 and left Hae in her car in the parking lot. They then drove to a spot in a state park and smoked a little weed before Wilds took Syed back to school. Wilds guessed that he dropped

Syed off sometime around 4:30 p.m. because the sun was going down.

Wilds returned home for a short time, until Syed called him for another ride. At some point Syed received a phone call from a police officer. Hae had already been reported as a missing person. Syed panicked and thought Hae's vehicle would be found where they left it, so they picked up a shovel from Wilds' house, retrieved Hae and her car, then drove to Leakin Park.

Wilds told detectives that Syed buried Hae face down in a shallow grave about 20 yards from where they parked. They then found a spot behind some row homes to hide Hae's car.

Police asked Wilds if he had talked to Syed about the actual murder. According to Wilds, Syed claimed to have strangled Hae to death in her car. Wilds also said that Syed had made threats against him to keep him from going to the police.

That's the gist of Wilds' statement anyway. The specific order of events and certain details changed over repeated tellings. In fact, during Wilds' first recorded interview, Detectives pointed out that the story he had told before the tape started rolling was significantly different than the one he told on record.

"During the first interview there were a lot of inconsistencies," Detective William Ritz said.

Wilds agreed.

"And there are too many to go over, but you kind of disassociated yourself from all of the information you provided in this interview," the detective continued.

Again, Wilds agreed.

"Why is that?"

"Scared," Wilds explained.

That was the first recorded statement.

Pretty good story, huh? I'd definitely read that book. But you know what would be fun? Let's take that book and adapt it for a screenplay. Only intellectuals read books, and we want to get this story out to the movie-going masses. First of all, Wilds' story lacks any real buildup to the murder. Syed just kind of springs the idea on Wilds at the mall that morning and then does it in the afternoon. Let's add a scene at Walmart the night before where Syed lays the groundwork for his motivation. And the meeting at a random spot on Edmondson? What a missed opportunity. Let's set it at Best Buy, maybe we can get some product placement dollars out of the deal. And there is a lot of wasted narrative between the murder and the burial. Maybe we should have Syed go to track practice to establish an alibi. And later they can hang out and smoke weed at a friends' house, so we can cast a few more attractive young people in speaking roles. Plus, Syed should give a chilling monologue about what a badass he is. The audience will respond to that. It's like Denzel in Training Day.

That's a good screenplay. Not a perfectly faithful adaptation of the source material, but it hits all the same major plot points. And it's unique enough to keep people interested even if they've already read the book. I love it. Unfortunately, it was from the second taped interview that Wilds gave in March. And it didn't stop. Each subsequent retelling seemed to have a few of those little twists and variations. Fine in fiction. But not what you are looking for in your key witness' statement.

I see that look on your face. This story's got more holes than my old jogging underwear. But we do have to acknowledge one gigantic thing that the story got right. After the first interview ended, Wilds went with the detectives and showed them exactly where Hae's car was!

That's how you establish credibility right there. You can get away with a pretty crazy story if you can back it up with corroboration like that. Wilds was involved with the murder in some capacity; no denying that much. But was he telling the truth about his involvement? And, more interestingly, was he telling the truth about Syed's involvement? Let's take a closer look.

Syed denied and still denies that he had anything to do with Hae's murder. Wilds said otherwise. At least one of them is lying. We should go point-by-point through each man's story and determine which seems more credible.

Wilds story: Syed killed Hae and buried her in a shallow grave in Leakin Park. Then he abandoned her car behind some row houses in Baltimore. Some stuff happened before that and after that, but the specifics evolve with each telling. And Wilds smoked a lot of marijuana that day.

Syed's story: Syed was probably at school and track practice that day. He doesn't remember any specific details, but he didn't kill Hae. And he smoked a lot of marijuana that day.

Well, that wasn't as productive as I'd hoped.

We have one story with a lot of unreliable details and one story with no meaningful details. You can't really compare and contrast stories like that. We'll have to find another way.

Let's go through the *Serial* evidence.

Syed told Koenig that he and Jay were not particularly close. They knew each other from school, but Jay wasn't in the magnet program. Syed was a close friend to Jay's girlfriend, Stephanie, but didn't hang out with Jay that much. He did buy weed from him occasionally, but they weren't best friends or anything.

All that said, Syed and Jay did hang out together during and after school on January 13. Syed was worried that Jay would forget to buy Stephanie a birthday present, so he lent Jay his car for the day so Jay could go to the mall.

I know, what a guy. He couldn't be a murderer. Turn that man loose.

Syed told Koenig he was in school for the rest of the day, went to the library afterward to check his email, then went to track practice until about 4:30 p.m. That is to say, he kind of told her that. He told her in a series of hypothetical statements like, "I would have," or "ordinarily" or "a lot of times I would..." but he never actually committed to any statement. At one point he said that he was "99-percent sure" that he didn't leave campus before the end of track practice, but that's as close as he got to an absolute. He was probably alive on January 13,

1999, he ordinarily would have been living in Baltimore, and he usually breathed oxygen. But he can't remember for certain.

Cynics view Syed's story as deliberately flexible. You can't call him a liar if you can't pin him to any specific facts. That's how you fish for an alibi if you don't actually have one. You leave yourself open to any alibi that develops. And of course, one did develop. After Syed was arrested for Hae's murder, a girl by the name of Asia McClain wrote him a couple of letters saying that she remembered seeing Syed in the library after school on January 13.

Since police said Syed was busy killing Hae after school, that is probably important information right? Syed's attorney didn't think so. She never bothered to contact Asia about her letters or try to introduce her claims in court.

Serial did most of an episode on Syed's original trial attorney, Tina Gutierrez. Listen to it if you haven't already. It's a fascinating story. She was locally famous and very accomplished. Health and personal problems seemed to have diminished her effectiveness by the time she took on the Syed case, but her reputation and track record masked a lot of things as they were happening. Syed's appellate attorneys argued that Gutierrez's performance was so deficient that Syed should have been entitled to another trial. But they argue that in every appeal whether it is true or not. You kind of have to if you want a shot at another trial.

Serial laid out a fairly convincing argument that Gutierrez may have dropped the ball with Asia McClain.

Whether you believe her or not, Asia was a potential alibi and Syed's attorney probably had a professional obligation to investigate her claims. But even in a diminished capacity, Gutierrez was no dummy. If she didn't think Asia's claims warranted further investigation, I have to believe she had her reasons. And I can think of a couple of them that show up on the face of the letters.

Asia started her first handwritten letter (just assume *sic* throughout, because I'm not editing this thing), "I know that you can't visiters, so I decided to write you a letter. I'm not sure if you remember talking to me in the library on Jan 13th, but I remembered chatting with you. Throughout you're actions that day I have reason to believe in your innocense. I went to your family's house and discussed your 'calm' manner towards them. I also called the Woodlawn Public Library and found that they have a survailance system inside the building. Depending on the amount of time you spend in the library that afternoon, it might help in your defense."

Later in the letter, she offered, "I'm trying to reach your lawyer to schedule a possible meeting with the three of us. We aren't really close friends, but I want you to look into my eyes and tell me of your innocense. If I ever find otherwise I will hunt you down and wip your ass, ok friend!! I hope that you're not guilty and I hope to death that you have nothing to do with it. If so I will try my best to help you account for some of your unwitnessed, unaccountable lost time (2:15 - 8:00 ; Jan 13th)."

So they aren't close friends, but she went and visited Syed's parents' house after he was locked in jail. She wants to sit down and have him "look into [her] eyes." If Syed had nothing to do with it, she will try her best to account for some of his previously unaccounted for time. And she lists a window of 2:15 p.m. until 8:00 p.m., even though there was no way that Syed was in the library for that length of time that day.

Gutierrez probably had a professional obligation to talk to Asia, but I don't blame her for not wanting Asia to show up in court. Regardless of how she actually intended it, the letter sounds like she is offering to fabricate an alibi for him if Syed looked in her eyes and promised he didn't do it. And it sounds like she had a schoolgirl crush on him.

The first letter was dated March 1, 1999, and she sent a second typewritten letter, dated March 2, 1999, as well. The second letter made it sound less like she was offering to fabricate an alibi, but more like she had a schoolgirl crush and was trying to insert herself into a situation she had nothing to do with.

Two revealing excerpts:

"It's weird, since I realized that I saw you in the public library that day, you've been on my mind. The conversation that we had, has been on my mind. Everything was cool that day, maybe if I would have stayed with you or something this entire situation could have been avoided. Did you cut school that day? Someone told me that you cut school to play video games at someone's house. Is that what you told the police? This entire case puzzles me, you see I have an analytical mind. I want to be a criminal psychologist for the FBI one day."

And, "You could attempt to write back though. So I can tell everyone how you're doing (and so I'll know too)." With a postscript after her name of "Apparently a whole bunch of girls were crying for you at the jail... Big Playa Playa (ha ha ha he he he)."

You know those people who always try to attach themselves to big events as a way to make themselves feel important? They flock to murder investigations. Any murder that makes the television news is probably going to have a handful of witnesses volunteering nonsense just to feel like they are a part of the investigation. I don't know Asia McClain and maybe she's not that type of person, but since she wrote a memoir to capitalize on her "fame" from the Serial podcast, I'm definitely not ruling it out.

More importantly, she wrote those letters in March. What are the odds that she remembered the specific day that she happened to see Syed almost two months after the fact? In the letters she said that she was not close with Syed or Hae. Syed said he was frequently in the library after school. Asia said her boyfriend picked her up from the library that day and saw Syed, but her boyfriend didn't remember it when Koenig talked to him (granted, that was years later).

Asia claimed that she was certain of the day because it snowed that night and school was cancelled the next day. Syed claimed he couldn't remember any details of that day because nothing out of the ordinary happened to him and it was a long time ago. A phone call from the police asking about his missing ex-girlfriend wasn't enough to make the day memorable for Syed. Snow in Baltimore in January was enough for Asia?

Everything about this scenario tells me that Asia had seen Syed in the library after school many times before and wanted so desperately to be a part of the biggest story going on in her world at the time that she convinced herself she remembered seeing Syed the day of the murder. You can do what you want with Asia's story, but I'm not putting any faith in it.

But even if every word she said was the truth, where would that get us? Would Syed at the library after school mean definitively that he could not have killed Hae? Let's go through a highly imprecise and convoluted timeline.

School got out for Hae and Syed at 2:15 p.m. Detectives theorized from Wilds' statement and Syed's cell phone records that Syed killed Hae by 2:36 p.m. Wilds also claimed that Syed called him from a pay phone in the Best Buy parking lot. Koenig and her producers did a really good job of recreating what it would take to pull off a murder in that timeframe and get to Best Buy. They concluded that it was possible, but very difficult. And that's not factoring in the risks of strangling somebody in broad daylight.

But that timeline is based off of two things that are really lacking in reliable detail: Jay Wilds' story and 1999 cell phone records. We've covered the problems with Wilds' story. So let's look at the trouble with the phone records.

AT&T cell phone bills in 1999 showed who outgoing calls were directed to but not where incoming calls originated from. So we can't even be certain that Syed's phone ever received a phone call that day from a payphone at Best Buy. There was an incoming call at 2:36 p.m., which was the basis of the state's timeline. But there were also incoming calls at 3:14 p.m., 4:27 p.m. and 4:58 p.m. Assuming Wilds was even telling the truth about his version of events, why couldn't either the 3:14 p.m. call or the 4:27 p.m. call have been from Syed after the murder? Either scenario would make Asia's letters irrelevant.

Various witnesses place Hae, Syed or both at the school anywhere from 2:15 p.m. to 3:15 p.m. It's really hard to put too much faith in any of them because so much time passed before those statements were given to police. Memory is fickle and unreliable, especially with details like that.

The 3:14 p.m. timeline would make it more difficult for Wilds and Syed to smoke the joint in the woods, stash Hae's car and get back in time for track practice. The 4:27 p.m. timeline would make it pretty much impossible. But the thing is, we don't really have anything to corroborate that Syed was actually at track practice that day. Wilds and Syed both say so, but if Syed killed Hae then of course he would lie about that. And Wilds' version is fluid enough that I don't know what to make of it. Syed's track coach said Syed was usually at track practice, but coaches didn't take attendance and he couldn't say for sure either way. Plus, because Syed was observing Ramadan and fasting, so he wasn't actively participating in practice at the time. If he showed up late, would anybody notice enough to remember?

If Syed really never left the school until after track practice, as he sort of claims, then there is a problem with his cell phone records. Wilds was using the phone most of the day, as shown through a series of calls that afternoon to Wilds' friends. But there was also a three-minute call at 3:32 p.m. to a girl named Nisha. Syed knew Nisha and called her frequently. Wilds didn't know her at all.

Nisha testified that she did not know Wilds, but that she had spoken to him on the phone one time. Syed called Nisha from his cell phone while he was at the video store where Wilds worked.

Well, it was a porno video store if we want to be precise, not that it makes any difference to the story. But you don't know me at all if you think I'm going to pass on a chance to point out a detail like that. That kind of information adds color to the story. Here's a tip for when you are writing your own crime book: if you have any scene set in a video store, go ahead and change it to a porno video store. It instantly makes your story 15% grittier and more authentic.

But anyway, Nisha said that Syed handed Wilds the phone and they spoke briefly about nothing in particular. But since Wilds hadn't gotten the job at the porno video store as of January 13, there is a decent chance that the phone call Nisha described wasn't the 3:32 p.m. call we are looking at. Nisha didn't remember that specific call, nor would we expect her to months after the fact.

Serial did the single most authoritative analysis you will ever hear on the mechanics of butt-dialing. It was heroic and groundbreaking investigative journalism. I'm not being sarcastic either, it was really exhaustive and interesting. Their conclusion: it is possible that the 3:32 p.m. call to Nisha was actually a butt-dial by Wilds. It's highly unlikely, but possible. AT&T didn't usually start billing for a phone call until somebody picked up on the other end, but acknowledged that in unusual circumstances, they did. If somebody let the phone ring for an excessively long time without an answer, they'd bill the caller. And three minutes fit the criteria for an excessively long time. Nisha did not have a voice mail account at the time, so it could have rung indefinitely. If the call was actually a butt-dial from Wilds, Nisha would have had to let it go for three minutes without answering and Wilds would have had to not notice the ringing sound in his pocket for three minutes.

Syed's phone was a Nokia 6160 cell phone, which did have the keys on the outside, so it's a more plausible scenario than it would have been with a flip phone. The phone did come with a keylock function to prevent butt-dials, but we have no way to know if it was active at that particular time. At any rate, there didn't seem to be any other butt dials on Syed's phone records on the morning or afternoon of January 13, so it was a pretty big fluke if it happened to be one.

AT&T figured prominently into the investigation. In addition to the call logs, they also provided records showing which cell phone towers were used for all the calls on Syed's log. One of those calls was believed to have come from Leakin Park and others appeared to come from locations that Wilds claimed to have been with Syed that night. But I don't feel comfortable hanging Syed with the tower records. Technology is at a place now where we can do a lot of really cool things with cell tower records, but it's incredibly complicated and not nearly as precise as you'd think. I'm going to guess it was far less dependable in 1999. Let's just say that the cell phone was definitely in Baltimore and leave it at that.

I've probably tipped my hand by now and I'm sure you already figured out which way I'm leaning. I am pretty certain that Syed killed Hae. Let me lay out why and you can correct me where I'm wrong.

Wilds knew where Hae's car was and he told Jennifer on the night of Hae's disappearance that Syed killed her. I can't envision any reasonable scenario where Wilds is not involved in the murder in some capacity. He took the police directly to the victim's car, which they hadn't been able to find in a month of searching. That is the one absolutely indisputable piece of concrete evidence in this entire case.

Wilds and Hae were, by all accounts, the most casual of acquaintances and Wilds had no reason whatsoever to kill her. But Syed did. He can spin it any way he wants now, but the bottom line is that Hae broke up with Syed just a couple of weeks before the murder. That's a motive to murder her, no matter how much Syed protests that the breakup didn't bother him. And I don't care how many character references come out of the woodwork to say

Syed wasn't that kind of guy, I'm not buying it. Show me any murderer and I'll find you five people to say he would never do that sort of thing. Syed was a 17-year-old boy. I was a 17-year-old boy once myself. I know there isn't a less rational or more impulsive animal on the planet than a teenage human boy. We should all be kept on leashes until we turn 30, for the good of society.

That's not to say that all teenage boys are murderers, or even violent. But it would be silly to rule him out because a bunch of people said he was a good boy.

So, according to Syed, he and Wilds were not particularly close and didn't spend that much time together. Wilds was mostly just a weed hookup who happened to be dating Syed's friend. And yet, the day Hae was murdered, a murder that Wilds was indisputably involved with in some capacity, Syed spent most of the day with him. Not only do I not see any reason why Wilds would have killed Hae on his own, it's even more perplexing to try and figure out how he could have done it without Syed's knowledge. They spent the entire freaking day together!

And it wasn't just Jennifer who had seen Wilds and Syed together that night, multiple independent witnesses saw them together. A girl, referred to by the pseudonym Cathy in the podcast, said that Syed and Wilds came over to her apartment and hung out for a while that night acting "sketchy." She barely knew Wilds and didn't know Syed, but they were both there and they were both clearly high.

Cathy told Koenig, "The phone rings and [Syed] hadn't said anything the whole time he had been there, so when he answers the phone, and he's saying 'What am I going to do? What am I gonna say? They're gonna come talk to me. What am I supposed to say?' And I remember him sounding very worried—concerned. This was—whatever was happening was not good on the other line."

From Cathy's description, it was in the ballpark of the time that Officer Adcock called Syed. But in fairness, nobody is precise enough in their memory to know who actually called Syed while he was at Cathy's apartment.

And speaking of imprecise memory, let's get back to the story Syed told Koenig. Syed himself described it as self-serving and convenient, as if acknowledging that with a laugh was somehow supposed to mitigate everything wrong with his version of events. He can say over and over again how sorry he is that he doesn't remember anything, but we don't have to buy it. He said it was such a typical day that nothing stood out to him. Ridiculous. A girl who broke up with him three weeks prior went missing and the police called him about it. That's a damn memorable day for anybody. It's insulting for him to suggest that we'd believe otherwise.

For me, his story fell apart the moment he started telling it. Why did he give his phone and car to Jay that day?

Syed's words, "Well, Stephanie was a very close friend of mine, as I mentioned. And I just kind of wanted to make sure that she also got a gift from [Jay], you know? She had mentioned to me that she was looking forward to getting a gift from him. She mentioned that she was really happy to get the gift that I gave her. So as I would with any friend, I just kind of went to check on that. I kind of had a feeling that maybe he didn't get her a gift. And I had free periods during school. So it was not abnormal for me to leave school to go do something and then come back. So I went to his house. And I asked him, did you happen to get a present for Stephanie? He said no. So I said, if you want to, you can drop me back off to school. You can borrow my car. And you can go to the mall and get her a gift or whatever. Then just come pick me up after track practice that day."

Are we being heartless cynics if we call that hogwash? Because it sure smells like it's been used to wash the hogs. Have you ever caught a toddler doing something they aren't supposed to do? It's funny how their explanation is always about how they were actually doing something really nice, but it just happens to look naughty. "I wasn't pulling the dog's ears, I was whispering something nice to him." "I wasn't hitting my brother, I was scaring a big spider away." "I wasn't scratching the paint, I was cleaning it." Syed wasn't laying the groundwork to get into Hae's car later in the day, he was just making sure a friend got a birthday present from her boyfriend.

Syed told Officer Adcock on the very first phone call, way back on January 13, that Hae was supposed to give him a ride after school. He denied that he ever said it when police asked him about it later, but another independent witness heard Syed ask Hae for a ride during school that day. I'm going with Officer Adcock and the other witness over the man who said he can't remember anything about that day except specific details that seem to benefit him.

I have so much respect for Koenig and her producers on this story. It's the kind of dedicated journalism that you just don't see very often, especially in crime reporting. They were thorough. They were fair. They were nuanced. They presented the facts with context but not an agenda. And they did it in an entertaining way. You can tell that Koenig is not only very smart, but also wise and discerning. Far more so than I am, I can assure you.

So I say this with some regret, but I have no idea how Koenig came to the conclusion she did. She finished *Serial* by saying that she was on the fence about Syed, but leaning toward his innocence. To me he looks so obviously guilty that I feel like I must be missing something. I had to listen to the podcast twice. I just don't get it. He was the only one in Hae's life who really had a reason to kill her, he spent the entire day with a man who was definitely involved in the murder, and his story is smelly garbage.

If I can offer one explanation, I will say that it is sometimes more difficult to spot a lie when it is being told directly to you. It's easier for us to see Syed as manipulative and dishonest because we weren't the ones talking to him. An interview is a relationship. There is empathy, there is trust and there are exchanges of very personal information. The interviewer isn't always in the best position to be skeptical when they are trying to forge that relationship. I know that I've done suspect interviews where I walked out of the room believing a pack of lies, only to have a colleague on the other side of the glass point out everything that was obvious to an impartial observer.

Of course, there is still the matter of what we do with Wilds. What was his involvement with the murder? His story doesn't smell much better than Syed's, and he has changed it quite a few times. Was he an accessory after the fact, or something more?

In Wilds' story, Syed is single-handedly responsible for the murder. Syed killed Hae, Syed carried Hae to the woods, Syed buried Hae, Syed threatened Wilds to stay quiet. All Wilds did was drive a car and move a few shovelfuls of dirt. Syed was the only bad guy, and Wilds was mostly just a confused and scared kid who was bullied into a minor role in the murder.

It worked, and kept Wilds out of prison.

I wish Syed would just come clean and tell what actually happened. I bet in his version, Wilds would take on a much bigger role in the murder. I doubt Syed's story would be completely accurate either, but at least between the two stories we'd probably be able to find some middle ground that resembled the truth. But that would require Syed to admit to participating in the murder, and he seems committed to his "innocent" story at this point. And since he's convinced quite a few people to believe him, I don't see him backing away from it any time soon. At least not until he has a legitimate shot at parole. He seems to care too much about how people perceive him to risk being known as a murderer *and* a liar.

So without Syed's side of the story, we are left to guess at the specifics of the murder. Is that speculative? Absolutely. Is it reckless? Maybe a little. Are we scared? Of course not. We didn't name this book *Cautiously Recited Boring Details About Murder*.

So since at least one witness saw Syed ask Hae for a ride after school, and he admitted as much to the police before he realized how incriminating it was, we can probably say that Syed was looking for a way to get into Hae's car that day. Was that to kill her or something less nefarious? He certainly wouldn't have been the first boy to come up with a convoluted excuse to spend time around his ex, hoping she might take him back. So let's look at the execution of his plan.

Lending his car to Wilds gave Syed a legitimate reason to ask Hae for a ride. And doing it so that Wilds could buy a present for his girlfriend might seem like a sweet gesture if Syed was trying to impress Hae. So I could see that as laying the groundwork for trying to win Hae back. Of course, he was also going to need a second person to help shuttle vehicles if he intended to kill Hae, so it might also have just been the prep work for a murder.

I can't see a similar dual purpose for leaving the phone with Wilds. That only strikes me as a way to communicate with a co-conspirator. Maybe Syed always left the phone in the glovebox, as he claimed, but that sounds like a stretch. People weren't glued to their cell phones in 1999 like they are now, but it was still an expensive toy that kids didn't just lend to anybody. I guess it's possible that cell phones weren't allowed in school back then. It still seems more likely that he would just turn it off and put it in his locker or backpack. The cell phone isn't proof that Syed planned on murdering Hae, but it at least points in that direction.

are up for it. It's a decision you base on more than just "they sell weed, they are down for any crime." Syed knew Wilds would help him dispose of Hae's body. Which tells me they'd discussed it before. And not in a superficial way. Whatever Wilds said in those talks was enough to convince Syed that Wilds would help him with a murder. And even if Wilds ultimately turned on him, Syed was right, Wilds did try to help him get away with murder.

Remember when we talked about that thing we didn't want to talk about? Hae's bra and skirt being hiked up, but there was no semen on or in her body. Sorry, I hate to bring it up again, but that is interesting to me. Of course it is possible that her clothes just got bunched up because she was dragged to the gravesite, but I don't think that's what happened. First of all, she would have had to have been dragged by her feet in order to move the skirt and bra up her body, and that is an awkward way to drag somebody. Also, I didn't see any mention of a drag trail at the crime scene or abrasions on Hae's back consistent with being dragged. She was a 130-pound girl, so it seems much more likely that she was probably just carried to the gravesite. Particularly if there were two people disposing of her body.

If we didn't already know everything that we know about Syed and Wilds, this would be the kind of detail that made me wonder about a stranger abduction. Hae was a beautiful teenage girl and that is, unfortunately, a logical target for a sexually-motivated killer. And although we would expect there to be signs of sexual assault if she were abducted by a stranger, that isn't always the case. There are documented cases of sexually-motivated killers who derive their satisfaction from the murder itself. Others have been known to stop short of rape because of either impotence or a fear of leaving incriminating evidence. So absent any other evidence, it's conceivable that Hae was the victim of a sexually-motivated killer.

But we have other evidence. And it points right to Syed and Wilds. And I think the information about Hae's undergarments is consistent with everything else we know. As impolite as this is to think about, is it really that hard to imagine a scenario where two teenage boys disposing of a murder victim would take a moment to look at her nude body? It's really unsettling, but it's definitely not beyond the realm of possibility.

And if Wilds participated in that type of thing, it makes sense that he never went to the police about the murder. Maybe he didn't commit the murder, but he still had a lot to be ashamed of. And that could also be why he wouldn't admit to helping Syed move Hae's body or bury her. The police knew how Hae's body was found. If Wilds admitted to moving and burying the body then he would also have to know about the skirt and bra. The police didn't call him out on it and Syed never contradicted him, so Wilds was able to pretend he didn't know.

So there we have it. Syed killed Hae by himself. It was sort of planned and sort of spontaneous. He'd discussed it with Wilds enough beforehand that he was confident Wilds would help him. And he was right, Wilds did help him dispose of the body and hide the evidence.

That seemed pretty simple and straightforward, didn't it? This was the easiest one we've had so far. It's kind of nice to have a slam-dunk every now and then, especially after all of the trouble we had on some of the other cases. But since this one is so easy and obvious, I suppose it's inevitable that some sort of evidence will come along in the future and completely exonerate Syed. That's how this world works. You're the most wrong when you're certain you're right.

In that spirit, I will point out that our solution does violate a couple of my basic rules for solving murders. First of all, I hate to put as much faith as we have in the story of a co-conspirator. Especially when there is no way to verify a lot of the specific details. And second, I hate when we don't have physical evidence that definitely ties the suspect to the crime. It's possible to build a convincing case entirely on circumstantial evidence, and the case against Syed is very convincing, but I'd still feel a lot better if we had something more reliable than the cell tower records tying him to Leakin Park that night.

But we can't have everything, and I'm comfortable calling this one solved until we learn otherwise.

Kathleen Peterson

Can we have an uncomfortable talk right off the bat? Don't get me wrong, I am grateful for everything you are contributing. But I don't feel like we are doing an equal share of the work here. I'm the one doing all of the research. I'm the one summarizing all of the facts. I'm the one formulating the theories, putting my reputation on the line. Sure, you come in and correct me when I'm wrong. And I appreciate that. But I might need a little more out of you this time. There are a lot of technical details in this case. There are high-dollar attorneys and Ph.Ds and Oscar-winning French documentarians. I might be in over my head.

So how about you do some of the heavy lifting on this one?

OK, I get it. You paid for the book. You don't have to keep throwing that in my face. I'm aware of our financial arrangement. Fine, I'll write this chapter too. But don't be shy about solving this thing. We are a team after all.

The problem here is that our job in every other case was to determine who committed a murder. That's enough of a job as it is. But we added a step on this one. First we have to determine if a murder actually took place. That was a given in every other case. No way to mistake the Tupac shooting or Kimberly Nees' beating for natural causes. But it's not so cut and dried with this one. There are smart people claiming it was clearly an accident and other smart people claiming it was clearly a murder. We have to figure out which smart people are wrong. That's rarely an easy thing to do, in and of itself.

And if we do determine that a murder took place, then we still have to figure out who did it. We just doubled our work, with no additional pay. Who negotiated this contract anyway?

Our sources on this case are going to be the book *A Perfect Husband* by Aphrodite Jones and the television miniseries/documentary *The Staircase* by Jean-Xavier de Lestrade. Contrary to what you may have guessed from the title, Jones' book is not about old Barney Doyle. The title is deliberately ironic because Jones believes the murder theory and you can probably deduce who she thinks committed it. Lestrade claims not to have an opinion either way, but his documentary skews heavily toward the accident theory. So our sources don't agree right off the bat, which is a fun way to start a new investigation.

We will also use a lot of information from filings made with the North Carolina Court of Appeals. Which, as you probably surmised, means that somebody was convicted of a crime. Sorry to give it away. Again, try to act surprised when you read about it in a few paragraphs.

The victim in this case was Kathleen Peterson. Without hyperbole, we can say that Kathleen was an incredible person. She was the first female to be accepted into Duke University's School of Engineering. She was an executive for one of the largest telecommunication companies in North America. She was a loving mother to one daughter of her own and four stepchildren. She was beloved and admired by many in the Durham North Carolina community where she lived. Murder or accident, her death was a tragedy that caused a lot of hurt to a lot of people.

On December 8, 2001, Kathleen and her husband, Michael Peterson, were home watching a movie on television. Michael's adult son, Todd Peterson, was at the house for a short time with a female friend, but Michael and Kathleen were otherwise alone. They were drinking champagne to celebrate the fact that one of the novels Michael had written was being considered for a movie. More on that later.

At 2:40 the following morning, Michael called 911 to report that Kathleen had fallen down the stairs. Michael told the dispatcher that she was breathing but unconscious. Michael pleaded for the operator to send medical attention, but hung up on them as they were speaking. He called back a couple of minutes later and asked where the ambulance was. He also said Kathleen had stopped breathing. The operator tried to ask additional questions, but Michael did not answer. Then he hung up again.

Paramedics arrived in approximately eight minutes and determined that Kathleen was dead. She was so clearly dead that they did not attempt to revive her. Michael was hysterical and crying. Todd Peterson returned to the home at essentially the same time as the paramedics arrived.

The paramedics later testified that Peterson was hunched over Kathleen when they arrived. He had blood on his hands, arms, legs and feet. The shorts and t-shirt he was wearing were also soaked in blood. Peterson told the paramedics that he had gone outside to turn off the lights, and when he returned he found Kathleen at the bottom of the stairs.

One of the paramedics testified that the amount of blood in the area seemed excessive for a fall and that blood on the wall appeared as if somebody had wiped it. The paramedic also testified that the blood under Kathleen's head had already clotted and started to harden.

Police arrived not long after paramedics and observed that Kathleen was laying at the bottom of the staircase with her head propped up on a roll of paper towels. There was a pair of flip-flops, a pair of men's tennis shoes and a pair of white socks on the floor near the body. Michael Peterson was barefoot.

Police found that there appeared to be blood smeared over already-dried blood on the walls of the stairway. They also saw blood on the soles of Kathleen's bare feet and a bloody shoe impression on the back of her pants, which was eventually matched to Peterson's shoe.

Michael Peterson displayed his grief outwardly and vocaly. At one point he hugged Kathleen's body and cried. That, of course, transferred more blood to his clothes and nullified the value of any trace evidence that might be found on Kathleen's body linking Peterson to her death in any way.

Todd's female friend from earlier was with him when he returned to the house, and two other friends showed up as well. Police had to separate them all as best they could so that they could be interviewed independently. Todd and Michael Peterson were upset at the way police were treating them and let it be known that they did not appreciate it. Ultimately they declined to give a statement to officers that night, correctly assuming that police believed Michael may have been involved with Kathleen's death.

While police were keeping Michael away from the crime scene, he was held in his home office. Police noted that he was on his computer checking his email to pass the time.

In addition to writing novels, Michael Peterson also wrote a regular column for the local newspaper. He frequently used that column to criticize the Durham Police Department. Michael and Todd both believed that the department was retaliating for the columns by treating Michael like a murder suspect in what was clearly an accidental death. They would convince most, but not all, of their family that the Durham Police Department was deliberately setting Michael up for murder to get revenge for his newspaper column.

On top of his writing career, Michael had also made two attempts to run for public office in Durham. He lost both bids, one for mayor and one for city council. But his writing career and the election campaigns had made him enough of a public figure that Peterson believed the police were targeting him.

A medical examiner responded to the scene and made a preliminary determination that Kathleen had died of an accidental fall. An autopsy was conducted later that day and found that Kathleen had seven lacerations to her skull and bruising on her arms. The medical examiner conducting the autopsy believed that the injuries were not consistent with an accidental fall and ruled Kathleen's death a homicide.

Police secured search warrants and kicked everybody out of the house for several days while they processed the scene. They discovered blood spatter high up on the walls of the staircase. They also found a drop of blood on the porch outside the back door. With the help of our old friend Luminol, they found a set of bloody footprints leading to the kitchen. The footprints were not visible to the naked eye, suggesting that somebody had cleaned them.

In a subsequent search warrant, police collected and analyzed the computer from Michael Peterson's office. They discovered that Michael had been corresponding with a male prostitute in the weeks leading up to Kathleen's death and was arranging to have sex with the man. The emails had been deleted, but were still recovered by the nerds... I mean the forensic computer examiners.

Police also probed the Petersons' finances. They found that although the Petersons lived a lavish lifestyle in a large expensive home, they appeared to be living beyond their means and accumulating a lot of debt. A forensic accountant determined that for the past couple of years the Petersons had been spending significantly more than they were making.

The large telecommunications company that Kathleen worked for was the Canadian company Nortel Networks. Let me refresh your memory on why that name sounds familiar. Nortel suffered one of the most high-profile corporate collapses ever in 2001. In 2000, Nortel was one of the largest telecommunication companies in the world and worth about $400 billion Canadian dollars. Then the dot-com bubble burst and the company laid off two-thirds of its workforce in 2001. The company was bankrupt by 2009.

Kathleen made a great salary but elected to take a large chunk of her compensation in Nortel stock rather than cash. It was working out great in 2000. On paper, she was a millionaire. But all of that stock became worthless almost overnight and she lost her entire nest egg. And at the time of this story, she was spending most of her days firing subordinates and wondering when her bosses were going to do the same to her.

Michael Peterson was a successful writer. He was reportedly paid about $600,000 for his second novel. That is a nice chunk of money right there. But that was published in 1990 and he had had no real success after that. The forensic accountants determined that he hadn't made money off of any of his books in the two years prior to Kathleen's death.

No money in books, huh? Interesting. That's a helluva thing to learn on the last chapter. Where was this information when we started this project?

The Durham Police called in assistance from the State Bureau of Investigation. Blood spatter expert Duane Deaver responded and examined the stairwell. He determined that the blood spatter on the walls was the result of Kathleen being struck in the head while she was standing on the stairs, not from striking her head on the stairs. Several years after the trial, it was learned that Deaver had a habit of making shit up to secure convictions. I think we are safe to disregard all of his opinions on the source of Kathleen's injuries. If he was right, it's just a coincidence. He was a blood spatter expert like I'm a forensic phrenologist.

On December 20, 2001, Michael Peterson was indicted for Kathleen's murder. At trial, the prosecution argued that Michael struck Kathleen multiple times in the head with a blunt object. They theorized a fireplace tool called a blow poke was used because it was the right shape and size and one was missing from the house. The defense pulled a gotcha moment in the trial and whipped out what they claimed was the missing blow poke (which even if it didn't violate the rules of discovery, certainly violated the spirit). The defense claimed that the blow poke was in the garage all along and that the police had just failed to find it. It played into the defense's general theme of the police being incompetent and vindictive.

The jury didn't buy it and Peterson was convicted of Kathleen's murder.

So why is this a complicated case? It looks pretty straightforward at this point. Peterson beat Kathleen to death with a blunt object. He tried to clean it up, but that didn't work, so he tried to make it look like an accident. The scene didn't match the accident he was staging, so he got caught. Pretty simple story. What's the controversy?

Enter *The Staircase*.

Lestrade won an Oscar for a documentary he made about a 15-year-old child wrongly accused of murder in Florida. He stayed in the genre for his follow up and decided to follow the Peterson case. Peterson and his attorneys allowed Lestrade to follow them everywhere short of the shower from the day of Peterson's arrest until his eventual conviction. He was also allowed to record the courtroom proceedings.

Lestrade claimed that his intention was never to learn the truth about what happened to Kathleen, but rather to follow how the criminal justice system worked for a wealthy white man in the United States. Just his luck, he picked the first instance in recorded American history of a wealthy white man getting convicted of a crime other than stealing from other wealthy white people.

While Lestrade may not have intended to learn the truth about Kathleen's death, viewers can be forgiven for mistaking his intentions. It felt like a documentary about Kathleen's death, not necessarily the criminal justice system. A lot of screen time was given to people who were presenting facts about her death. And since Lestrade's access was through Peterson's defense team, those facts may not have painted the most complete picture.

The Staircase presented a series of witnesses who portrayed Michael and Kathleen as having a storybook marriage, interpreted the forensic evidence to show that Kathleen's death was accidental, and accused the police and prosecutors of malicious misconduct

According to the documentary, Michael was a loving husband and devoted father who could not be capable of murder. Michael and Kathleen had each been divorced once prior to their marriage and assembled a happy blended family. Michael had two sons with his first wife and two adopted daughters. Kathleen had one daughter of her own. Almost all of the children appeared prominently in the documentary to talk about how the police were framing Michael and how he wasn't capable of murder.

Almost all of the children appeared prominently, but one didn't. The documentary glosses over the fact that Kathleen's daughter absolutely believed Michael killed her mother. She didn't believe so initially, but after comparing the facts of the case to what she knew of Michael, she concluded that Michael had killed her mother. She loved him like a father, but saw enough of his temper and mood swings to know that he was not everything the other children were describing him as.

It should be noted that Kathleen's daughter grew up in the house with Michael, while Michael's boys grew up in Germany with their biological mother and did not move to the United States until after high school. It should also be noted that Michael's oldest son, Clayton Peterson, was convicted of placing a pipe bomb in an administration building at Duke University in 1994 and was sentenced to four years in federal prison. That's the kind of information that seems relevant to a witness's credibility. Especially when they are accusing the police of lying about something. That seems like a pretty deliberate and misleading omission on Lestrade's part.

The other two daughters are where the story gets really interesting. Michael became the girls' legal guardian when they were small children growing up in a United States military family in Germany. Michael and his first wife were living in Germany at the time and were close friends of the girls' parents. The girls' father died of an illness while on an overseas mission. The girls' mother died of an accidental fall.

It was an accidental fall down a staircase.

Witnesses described a suspicious amount of blood at the scene.

Michael was among several friends and neighbors at the house when police arrived and he actually helped clean up the blood so the girls wouldn't have to see it. German authorities ruled the death an accident, and Michael and his first wife became the girls' legal guardians.

When police in North Carolina found out about this story they had the exact same reaction you just did. Did Michael kill her? Well, possibly, but there is no way to know this long after the fact. The body was exhumed and a second autopsy determined that the injuries to the woman's head were not consistent with a fall and that the cause of death should have been ruled a murder. A witness in Germany claimed to have seen Michael running from the woman's house on the morning the victim was discovered, but that witness never actually testified to the statement in a court of law.

Peterson was a documented philanderer. He cheated on his first wife with Kathleen. He admitted to having sex with other men while married to Kathleen. It is conceivable that Peterson was having an affair with the victim in Germany, but there is no evidence to prove it.

Peterson was also rumored to be heavily involved in administering the victim's finances after her husband's death because she was overcome with grief. This was before Peterson found any success as a writer, so there could be some financial motive also. But we can't know for sure three decades after the fact.

At any rate, it's damn bizarre. How many people do you know who have died from falling down the stairs? I knew the answer before you said it. Zero. Same as my answer. It is a really unusual way to die. And the people who do die from falls are usually elderly or intoxicated. If you believe Peterson, two people who were extremely close to him both died from accidental falls down a staircase even though both people were young and healthy. That is an unbelievable coincidence. And I don't mean "unbelievable" in the way a football announcer uses the term on a long third down conversion. I mean I don't believe it.

The documentary did try to suggest that Kathleen was heavily intoxicated, but an autopsy showed she only had a blood-alcohol concentration of .07. That's below the legal limit for driving a car. That is a long way from being heavily intoxicated. That's giggling and dancing not stumbling and falling. The defense tried to argue that the Valium in her system compounded the effects of the alcohol, but that's a convenient and untestable claim.

The defense also tried to show that the prosecution was interpreting the evidence at the crime scene incorrectly. They argued that Deaver wasn't qualified to make judgments on the blood spatter evidence and that the work he did lacked scientific merit. Time would prove them correct on both counts. They then introduced renowned criminologist Dr. Henry Lee, who told the jury that the blood spatter was actually proof that Kathleen died from an accidental fall.

Forensic science doesn't refer to a specific discipline like physics or biology or chemistry or astronomy. It has elements of all of those things, but it often lacks the foundation that those disciplines built through centuries of the scientific method. The term literally means science for court. And like everything else for court, forensic science has its share of charlatans and snake oil salesmen looking to turn a buck on the judicial process.

I remember observing a conversation where prosecutors were discussing the need to hire one particular expert before the defense was able to. In theory it shouldn't matter who hired the expert. He should have just reviewed the facts and given his honest opinion based on the details of the case and his knowledge of the science. But that ain't the way this game works. In practice, experts take their paycheck and say whatever the hell they are paid to say.

Case in point, Dr Henry Lee. It's probably sacrilege for me to speak ill of Dr. Lee at this point, but what the hell. He's got enough people blowing smoke up his ass, he can deal with one claiming the emperor has no clothes.

Dr. Lee is by many accounts, including his own, the world's foremost "criminologist." And "criminologist" is a nebulous term that seems to signify "expert on all things criminal." As the world's foremost expert on all things criminal, Dr. Lee gets paid handsomely to give his opinions in court. He is articulate and charming and jurors love him. He is the picture of credibility on the stand. But is it earned? Well, the man got up on the witness stand in the OJ Simpson trial and said the evidence suggested there were at least two killers, neither of them being Simpson. Everybody else investigating the case believed it was OJ who committed the murders by himself. But as the world's foremost criminologist, Dr. Lee could read the crime scene in ways that nobody else could.

Dr. Lee was, of course, spectacularly wrong. OJ did it, by himself, and for a trained "criminologist" to say otherwise means that said "criminologist" is either terrible at his job or willing to say whatever he needs to collect a paycheck.

So while Dr. Lee may insist that the blood spatter is proof of a fall, I'm going to suggest that the blood spatter in that stairwell could say a lot of different things, depending on who is signing the paycheck.

I don't mean to imply that experts are all charlatans. They are not. They are super important to solving murders because you and I can't be experts on medicine, and biology, and physics, and computers, and psychology, and automobiles, and tool marks, and ballistics, and ornithology and the hundreds of other areas of knowledge that might come into play on any given murder. We need experts in these fields to explain the significance of certain evidence. But it's OK for us to question what they say. Part of being an expert is understanding your field well enough that you can explain the important concepts in a way that any reasonably intelligent layperson will understand. By this point in the partnership, I know you are an intelligent person. If you can't understand how an expert could possibly know what they are claiming to know, then they might not be as much of an expert as they are claiming. And it is OK to question what they are telling you and who is paying them to say it.

Police found spatter on the wall significantly above Kathleen's standing height. It could be, as Dr. Lee argued, deposited from Kathleen coughing with blood in her throat while lying on her back at the bottom of the stairs. It would take a tremendously powerful cough for somebody in the process of dying, but we can't rule it out. Or it could be, as Deaver said, cast off from the weapon that Kathleen's killer used to beat her. In a vacuum, either is a possible explanation. But we don't examine each piece of evidence in a vacuum. It needs context to have any meaning.

Kathleen had seven major lacerations to the back of her head. She didn't fall and hit her head seven times. This isn't Looney Tunes. When Sylvester is chasing Tweety Bird and slips on the stairs, he bounces his head off of every step from the top to the bottom. When human beings fall, they try to catch themselves. If they get knocked unconscious, they go limp and come to a rest wherever gravity dictates.

If Kathleen fell at the top of the steps, we would expect for her to try to catch herself. She would have injuries to her arms from trying to brace her fall, maybe a broken leg or hip, and a knot on her head if she smacked it on something. But at her age she would almost certainly survive. If she couldn't catch herself for some reason, then maybe we'd see one or two massive skull injuries that might have killed her. But not seven.

Realistically, if she was dead from an accidental fall down the stairs we would expect to find a broken neck. But there was no broken neck. There were contusions and abrasions to her head, neck, arms, wrists and hands, but nothing fatal. The injuries to the arms could be evidence that Kathleen really did fall and try to catch herself. But if that were the case then there would be no reason whatsoever why she should have suffered seven lacerations to the back of the head and died in the fall. The injuries could also be defensive wounds if she was trying to protect herself from an attack.

The crime scene technicians indicated that there were transfers of blood over the top of already-dried blood on the wall. Logically that would suggest that Kathleen was murdered. A killer could brush against the wall in a hundred different ways and transfer blood. But how could Kathleen transfer blood to the wall if she was already down? The defense theorized that Kathleen stood up after falling to the bottom of the stairs, then slipped on her own blood and fell back down again. If it wasn't so unbelievably disrespectful to a dead domestic violence victim, I could almost respect the Three Stooges analysis. But as an actual explanation, I don't buy it.

The documentary would also lead you to believe that the murder accusation came out after the fact. The documentary makes it sound like the people who got to the scene first believed it was an accident. And they were in the best position to evaluate everything. They saw the scene undisturbed. They saw Michael Peterson's reaction firsthand. They got the first bite at the apple, so to speak. And the medical examiner who responded to the scene made an initial ruling that the death was an accident.

The documentary makes it seem as if the first medical examiner was pressured to change his ruling by police who wanted to manufacture a murder charge. He was pressured, but not by police or prosecutors. He was pressured by the evidence. There was no way to see all of Kathleen's injuries without an autopsy. But once he saw all of those injuries, there was no way to ignore the obvious. He made a judicious decision at the scene not to jump to conclusions and ring a murder bell that can't be un-rung. When he had better information he gave a better answer. There is nothing sinister about that.

And the other people who responded to the scene were far from convinced that the death was an accident. Almost everybody testified that there was a shocking amount of blood, more than could reasonably be expected from a fall. That alone was enough to make people suspicious.

Plus, the one thing that the documentary could not hide was that Michael Peterson was a peculiar dude. He had an intense way of speaking that made everything he said seem like a performance. Even when he told the truth he didn't seem believable. But you and I both know that kind of analysis is bunk and that the only real way to know if somebody is lying is to compare what they say to the known facts. So let's do that.

Michael claimed that he was sitting out at the pool by himself and didn't know how long Kathleen had been laying at the bottom of the staircase when he found her. But the paramedic who responded to the house testified that Michael told him he just went outside to turn off the lights and came back into the house to find Kathleen at the bottom of the stairs.

Peterson claimed in his initial 911 call that Kathleen was still breathing, then called back a couple of minutes later to say that she had stopped. The initial responders testified that the blood under her head was already clotted and hardening when they arrived less than 8 minutes later and that she appeared to have been dead for a while.

Peterson claimed he and Kathleen were celebrating because one of his novels was going to be turned into a movie. He also claimed they were not having financial difficulties, but even if they were, his ship was about to come in. Kathleen's daughter pointed out that Peterson had said many times before that his book was being made into a movie, but it never materialized. Kathleen's sister said Kathleen confided in her that she and Michael were having serious financial troubles. The state's financial examiner reported the Petersons had been spending drastically more money than they made for years and had racked up considerable debt. The state also asserted Peterson stood to make almost $1 million in life insurance, deferred compensation and accumulated assets if Kathleen's death was ruled accidental but would receive nothing if he murdered her.

Peterson claimed Kathleen was aware that he had been having sex with other men and that she was OK with it. Kathleen's family insisted she was devastated by infidelity in her first marriage and would not have tolerated it from Peterson. The state also showed evidence that Kathleen used Michael's computer to receive a work email the night she died and that the computer in Michael's office held evidence of his attempts to hire the prostitute. Michael insisted Kathleen already knew about that and would not have cared.

Police say they searched the house up and down multiple times, including the garage, and never found a blow poke. Michael Peterson said he stumbled onto it in the garage while looking for something else. Prosecutor Jim Hardin was contacted toward the end of the trial from a woman in Maine who said a man named Michael

Peterson had ordered three blow pokes from her. Peterson's attorney had already presented the blow poke in court before the woman shipped those, but it is curious that a man named Michael Peterson was in the market for blow pokes at the same time that a man named Michael Peterson desperately needed one for a murder trial. I'd never even heard of a blow poke before this case.

The general theme of all of this is that independent witnesses make a lot of claims that implicate Peterson and directly contradict what Peterson was saying. So who should we believe? Well, for what it's worth, Peterson was a well-documented liar long before Kathleen died.

Peterson was a Vietnam veteran who claimed to have won multiple Purple Hearts for his service. But the local media started doing due diligence when he was running for public office and discovered that he'd never received any Purple Hearts. He first claimed that he lost the paperwork and misplaced the medals. But eventually he admitted that he was actually injured in a car crash in Japan that had nothing to do with combat and never received a Purple Heart. He didn't elaborate on his lies because his time in Vietnam was too traumatic for him to relive it. Bear in mind that his novel was about the Vietnam war. But apparently some fiction is easier to discuss than others.

I think we've seen enough to throw out a guess on this case.

Kathleen's death was a murder. Michael Peterson killed Kathleen Peterson. He beat her to death with some hard object, possibly a blow poke, then tried to stage the scene to look like an accidental fall. He cleaned up what he could, but not well enough. He then placed a couple of carefully worded 911 calls that ultimately convinced nobody.

The real interesting question for me is whether or not the murder was planned or a spontaneous outburst of domestic violence. Most people who knew Michael said he could be moody with flashes of anger, but almost nobody said he was violent. Kathleen had confided in her sister about one instance of violence, but it fell well short of murder. Most domestic murders are not planned, but most domestic murders come with a documented trail of violence leading to the murder.

I think he planned the murder. I think he was a lavish spender who wanted to appear wealthy, and was getting desperate about their financial situation. I think that Kathleen either suspected or knew about his infidelity and that the marriage was threatening to implode. I think he had a loose plan about how he would murder Kathleen, but something that night set the plan in motion. She probably discovered something on his computer when she was checking her email.

The location of the attack is what makes me think it was premeditated. He knew firsthand that a murder could be mistaken for a fall down the stairs. If it was done in a fit of rage, odds are it would have happened in a place they spent more time at than the staircase. If he killed her in the living room or on the patio and moved her body to the bottom of the stairs, he couldn't have cleaned the scene well enough to hide the telltale trace evidence. He wasn't even able to wipe up his bloody footprints well enough to hide that. He attacked her in the staircase for a reason. He staged it as best he could, but he wasn't quite as smart as he imagined himself to be.

And for what it's worth, I think he had something to do with the death in Germany as well. But there aren't enough reliable details about that death for me to really support the theory. It just fits with the general pattern of what we know about Michael Peterson. He's now a convicted murderer. He was in the general area at the time and was close to the victim. It matches most of the details of the murder Peterson was convicted of. It walks like a duck, it quacks like a duck, I'm calling it a duck.

Speaking of birds, we'd be doing a great disservice to ourselves if we didn't take a moment to make fun of the famous owl theory that has been circulating around this case. One of Peterson's neighbors, who happened to be an attorney, was reading documents associated with the case when he observed that a microscopic owl feather and a sliver of wood were found in a clump of Kathleen's hair that was in her hand and had been pulled out by the roots. Kathleen had long hair and regularly sat outside by the pool, so a microscopic feather and sliver of wood could easily end up in her hair from the trees overhead or the chair she was sitting on. There are microscopic traces of rat feces in most fast food hamburgers, but we usually assume the cow was killed by a butcher and not necessarily the rat. But a homicidal owl makes for a much better story.

Well, shoot. That was an option all along? I assumed we were supposed to be reasonable about this. But if we're going with a murderous owl for Kathleen's death then I want to change my vote on a couple of the other ones:

Teresa Halbach was a tragic case of spontaneous human combustion.

JonBenét was killed by Bigfoot. The monster truck, not the mythical ape-man.

Tupac and Biggie were taken out by time-traveling cyborgs from the year 2075.

Kimberly Nees is still alive and working deep undercover for the CIA.

Hae Min Lee was killed by the government because she learned the truth about Kimberly Nees.

On a more serious note, I like that we finished this entire thing off with Peterson and started it with Steven Avery. Out of every case in this book, I am most confident in those two. It's nice to have a dunker on both ends of this thing to make us feel smart.

But they also seem to be the two who have convinced the most people of their innocence.

How is that?

First of all, they both have relatively flattering Netflix documentaries about them. Second, they each claimed the local police had a vendetta against them. That's a pretty simple formula really. I don't want you to ever kill anybody, but just in case you have to, go ahead and befriend a talented film student now. And maybe insult your local sheriff a few times, just to be safe.

Conclusion

That was quite a ride you and I went on right there. We just solved seven of the most controversial famous murders of our time. And we did it from the comfort of our couches. That's impressive work.

Of course, we didn't agree on a lot of it. Or maybe any of it. But we got through it nonetheless. I think it's a better book for our disagreements, actually. Debate is a healthy way to get to the truth.

I can't wait to see the epilogue on the second printing, ten years from now, when I have to admit that you, the amateur true crime enthusiast, were correct on all seven cases while I, the trained homicide investigator, whiffed on every one. It will fit nicely with the theme of this book. Or themes, I guess I should say. Those being: 1. You can make educated guesses from limited information, but you can't be certain without all of the facts; and 2. Barney Doyle is a braying jackass who can't spell two-syllable words.

While we finish up, I thought I should take a moment to highlight the things that I think are most important about the work we just did. First of all, every one of these murders was a tragedy and the victims deserved so much better out of life. Second, each one of these murderers was an absolute piece of shit who deserves nothing but our mockery and contempt. Third, you are far less likely to come to a bad conclusion if you base it on solid facts. Fourth, a fact isn't solid until you can corroborate it in a meaningful way. Fifth, people lie, but it isn't always easy to tell when they are doing it. Sixth, it's OK to be skeptical of experts, especially when they are claiming to know things that don't seem knowable.

And lastly, you and that book-spending-money of yours are welcome to solve murders with me anytime.